# ADVENTURE WALKS

D1386619

# FOR FAMILIES
## in and around London

# ADVENTURE WALKS

# FOR

# FAMILIES

## in and around
## London

Becky Jones & Clare Lewis

**F**

FRANCES LINCOLN LIMITED
PUBLISHERS

We would like to dedicate this book with much love to our husbands, David and Guy, and our children, Edward, Alex, Isabella, Harry, Ottoline and Freddie.

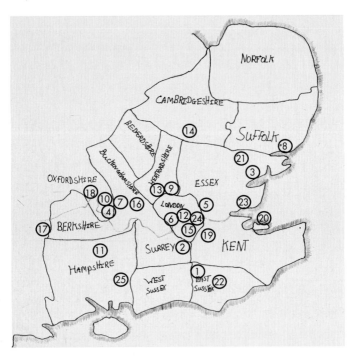

Frances Lincoln Ltd
4 Torriano Mews
Torriano Avenue
London NW5 2RZ
www.franceslincoln.com

Adventure walks for families in and around London
Copyright © Frances Lincoln 2008
Text and photographs © Becky Jones and Clare Lewis
2008 except p144 photograph © English Heritage
Photo Library
Walk maps by Frances Bennett
Contents map and illustrations by the Martin (Lewis)
children, Edward aged 10, Isabella aged 8, Ottoline
aged 6, and the Crichton-Miller (Jones) children, Alex
aged 10, Harry aged 8, and Freddie aged 4

First Frances Lincoln edition: 2008

A catalogue record for this book is available from the British Library.

ISBN: 978-0-7112-2752-1

Printed and bound in China

9 8 7 6 5 4 3 2

Ladybird

# contents

There never was a child but has hunted gold, and been a pirate,
and a military commander, and a bandit of the mountains;
but has fought, and suffered shipwreck and poison, and imbrued
its little hands in gore, and gallantly retrieved the lost battle,
and triumphantly protected innocence and beauty.

Robert Louis Stevenson

# Introduction

We have written this book because we love the
outdoors and, like most London families, don't get the
opportunity to enjoy it as much as we'd like. We want
our children to learn how to play, get muddy, run wild,
climb hills and recognise birds, bugs, trees and flowers of the
countryside. So we have put together twenty-five walks that are
totally manageable for families, which are all within easy reach of
London and a few that are London-based.

As parents, we know when faced with the inevitable battles
about the PlayStation versus the not so obvious pleasures of playing
outside, it is often easier to retreat to the safety of the swings at the
local park or the swimming pool rather than venture out into the
countryside. In reality, who has the time to plan idyllic weekend
outings? As we found out when researching the book, it takes a lot
of getting it wrong to get it right. What we have done is to provide
you with great places to visit with heaps of things to do when you
get there, whilst making sure you have with you all the things you
are going to need once you have arrived.

Each walk has been inspired by a theme
such as castles, beaches, birds, or a favourite
children's book, using the characters of the
story and the location to fire the imagination.
These have all been devised as 'outdoor
adventures'. On each walk there is always

oystercatcher

something to see, draw, collect or visit. We have dipped into our own childhoods to find fun and diverting things to do, that cost nothing and are readily available in the wild. We have drawn up lists of things to take with you, diversionary games to play on the way, devised scavenger hunts, and sourced relevant story CDs to listen to in the car.

Much of the content of the book will be familiar to you; the point is that we've put it all together in one place. If, like us, you are prone to forgetting the words to songs or the name of a particular wild flower or are short of suggestions, we've written a few of them down. We have tried to cover all the questions that grown-ups and children are likely to ask: where are we going? How long will it take? What is there to do when we get there? What do I need to bring? Basically we have tried to provide a step-by-step guide for a fantastic free day in the country.

It works well to start the adventures before even leaving home: children are naturally interested in new things, and you may even see a flicker of enthusiasm about the day ahead if they are involved in the process. Each adventure requires some kind of kit, most of which you may already have, whether it's a crabbing line, a pocket knife, binoculars, first aid kit or a plastic sword (see page 10 for our Essential Walk Pack). Ask the children to gather together what you are going to need and stuff it in a backpack. Persist with this attitude; it can completely turn the mood of the day.

To get the best out of this book you probably need to read it right through as it is packed full of suggestions for games, activities and diversionary tactics. These are scattered through the chapters where we think they work best; however, many of them are generic so pick and mix as you go along. Each walk has a suggestion or two of good places to eat or whether to take a picnic. We just mention places we have been to and like. The illustrated maps are not to scale and are a rough guide, so we recommend you take along the relevant Ordnance Survey map too (available

comon whelk

8

from www.ordnancesurvey.co.uk/getamap).

To help make a walk a success, give everyone a turn at being the leader, have a grown-up who always walks at the pace of the slowest, and remember to take regular stops for a 'scroggin' snack (see recipe on page 10) or a drink. There will be times when everyone needs a bit of extra encouragement to get them up the hill or back to the car at the end of a long day. A bag of sweets is often invaluable, handed out only when desperate so you don't run out too soon. Diversionary tactics and good old entertainment also work a treat (see suggestions on page 11).

Above all, these family rambles provide the much-needed benefits of fresh air and exercise that for urban children are in such short supply, encouraging resourcefulness and responsibility, and an awareness of the environment. More importantly, they introduce children to the freedom of the great outdoors. Don't make a big deal out of it, just hop in the car and go.

## ESSENTIAL WALK PACK

- Water
- Snacks
- First aid kit with plasters and bite and sting cream or spray
- Plastic bags or small boxes for storing finds
- Camera
- Fishing line and hook
- Nets or old sieves for pond dipping
- Notebook and pencil
- A whistle – in case someone gets lost
- Garden scissors
- String
- Magnifying glass
- Pocket knife
- Torch
- Compass
- Bug box
- Wellington boots
- A picnic rug

If you are walking in the woods, you might want to bring a small, foldable handsaw for cutting wood and a thick pair of gloves. It makes things like shelter building, foraging for food and general mucking about much easier.

### 'SCROGGIN' RECIPE

A New Zealand high-energy snack that you put together yourselves. Mix together raisins, sultanas, nuts, chocolate (Smarties or chocolate buttons are good), dried fruits, seeds and toasted oats in any combination you like. Give everyone their own bag and munch as you go.

## DIVERSIONARY TACTICS

- Make up stories as you go along: put your child in as the hero/heroine; take it in turns to add the next sentence
- Tell tales about when you were young . . .
- Make up silly walks.
- Play follow my leader. Take it in turns to be in the lead and do actions that everyone has to copy.
- Sing songs.
- Stop for a breather and draw something together like a pine cone, or do a scavenger hunt (see pages 78 and 163).
- Go on a bear hunt.
- Play hide and seek.
- Send the kids ahead to ambush you.
- Shoot a short film.
- Give the children the camera to take pictures with.
- Theme your walk:
  a listening walk – stop, keep silent and see what you can hear;
  a shape walk – find things that are a certain shape;
  a 'smelly' walk – see how many different smells you can find and identify.

# 1. Winnie-the-Pooh and the Enchanted Forest

Ashdown Forest, High Weald, East Sussex

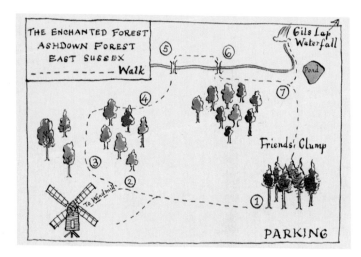

## The Adventure

Sing Ho! for the life of a bear. Head down to the Ashdown Forest, just south of the M25, into a wilderness of woods and open heath. This is where A.A. Milne wrote the Winnie-the-Pooh stories. Walk through the real Hundred Acre Wood and play Poohsticks at a stream, but avoid the hoards of tourists that inevitably descend on the official Pooh sights in one small corner of the forest.

We have found a quieter corner for our walk with its own small wood (Friends' Clump), a fabulous windmill, a small waterfall and a wooden bridge over a stream for Poohsticks. The walk starts at a clump of Scots pine trees just like the ones drawn by E.H. Shepard in the Pooh stories. Let yourselves get carried away with the Winnie-the-Pooh adventure. Gather sticks for Poohsticks, hunt for heffalumps in the woods, set a trap for woozles. Gather pine cones and build Eeyore's house. Make up Pooh-ish songs as you walk along. Set off on an expedition to discover the North Pole. Tiddly-pom.

It is a beautiful place to be. The Ashdown Forest, in spite of its name, is mostly open heathland, with rolling valleys and great views. And it is just as you would imagine, as if you are walking through the drawings in the Winnie-the-Pooh books. Rumour has it that some wallabies escaped from a captive colony and once roamed the forests. Perhaps a sighting of Kanga is still possible.

**Map** Ordnance Survey Explorer Map 135

**Distance** 3 km / 2 miles to the waterfall and back

**Terrain** This is an easy downhill walk to a stream, looping back up to Friends' Clump. Open heathland with a small wood at the bottom of the valley, running alongside a stream to a charming, small waterfall. It can be very muddy.

### What will I need?
- Pack honey sandwiches and honey cakes in your picnic.
- A book of Pooh stories and poems. Read aloud the chapter 'An Expotition to the North Pole' while you are there.
- A teddy bear
- Binoculars
- Fishing net and jars for pond dipping
- A sketch book for E.H. Shepard-style drawings

### How to get there
Take the M25 to Junction 6 where you turn off and follow the A22 (direction Eastbourne) to East Grinstead. Stay on the A22 through Forest Row, Wych Cross and past the Ashdown Forest Llama Park. After a mile or two, at Nutley, take the next small

turning on the left, signposted Crowborough. Drive up the hill and over the cattle grid. Turn left into the first car park called Friends' Clump.

## What can we listen to on the way?
- *Winnie-the-Pooh* read by Alan Bennett (BBC)
- *The Many Songs of Winnie-the-Pooh* for all the great songs from the classic Disney Pooh (Disney)
- *Winnie-the-Pooh*, *The House at Pooh Corner* and *Now we are Six* boxed set (K-Tel)
- *Winnie-the-Pooh* read by Peter Dennis (Blackstone Audiobooks)

## Walk the Walk
1 Take the path in front of the clump of trees down to the left, heading straight down the hill towards the woods.
2 There is a great windmill off to the left if you feel like a quick detour. Nutley Windmill is only open on the last Sunday of the

month but is worth a look open or closed. Otherwise stick to the main track, ignoring the right-hand path that curves down before the woods.

**3** Get back on the main track and keep following it through the trees, ignoring any minor turns to the left and right. Just before the path starts to descend, keep to the right. Ignore the left fork here.

**4** At the bottom of the valley, as the path levels off, follow it round to the right and then to the left, through some silver birch trees, towards a small brook.

**5** Cross at the wooden footbridge ahead of you. Turn right, scrambling along the left bank of the stream. It soon becomes a much easier bank to walk along, if a little muddy. In spring this riverbank is full of wild daffodils, in late spring, bluebells and in summer, foxgloves. The banks are gorgeously soft, mossy and green. It is a good spot for playing, exploring, pond dipping and adventures. As Christopher Robin would say, it is just the sort of place for an ambush.

**6** Before too long, cross back over to the other side of the stream (a sign says Keep Out: Property of the Ministry of Defence) over another narrow wooden footbridge. This is a good place for mini Poohsticks.

Carry on along the path, following the direction of the yellow arrow, this time with the stream on your left. Make your own path straight ahead, alongside the stream. The path starts to climb a little, leaving the stream below, but still travelling parallel to it. Follow it higher into the trees until it becomes a good, clear path,

### BUG HUNT

Organise a bug hunt; see how many different kinds you can find. A good place to search is under rocks, logs and leaves but always remember to cover the bugs back up after you've looked.

heading straight on. You are now in a wood of silver birch, beech and rowan trees. Look out for trees that could be Owl's house. And for Rabbit's house in the soft earth under foot.

As the path starts to climb, it splits left and right. Take the left-hand path, still parallel to the stream, but now way above it in the woods. The path comes out on to a wide bridleway, or firebreak. Keep going straight on. Friends' Clump is now on the hill to your right. Continue until the path dips down to a small pond. Good for a rest and a small smackeral of something.

**7** If you want to head back at this point, turn right and follow the wide track up the hill to Friends' Clump.

**For a longer walk**, turn left here and take the wide and open path to the left of the pond, heading straight on, for about 15 minutes. You are walking just above the stream and woods. As the path dips down to a small wooden footbridge, listen out for the sound of the waterfall and cut left into the woods in search of it. It is very small but charming. It is just the kind of waterfall that Roo went over when he fell into the stream on their Expotition to the North Pole. If you want to carry on

silver birch

## HAVE A WOODLOUSE RACE

A woodland is a good place for a break. Have a hunt for woodlice. These completely harmless creatures can be found under fallen branches, logs and old piles of rotting leaves, hiding from the daylight. Trap them carefully in your matchboxes, giving them names if you like (Schumacher, Speedy, Hamilton). Create three race courses by clearing three areas in the earth, all of similar shape and size. Gently tip the racing woodlice into the centre of each area, still trapped under the matchbox. On the count of three (or ready, steady, go), lift the lid and see which creature gets to the edge first.

walking, the wide path takes you further into the forest and eventually to Gil's Lap. Make sure you have the Ordnance Survey map with you.

When you are ready, head back, but this time scramble along small paths by the stream all the way back to the small pond. From here walk straight ahead, on a wide path out on to open heath covered with gorse bushes and purple heather and up to the top of Friends' Clump, something very like Christopher Robin's Enchanted Place. Look back at the long views behind you. Ahead of Friends' Clump are equally stunning views of the South Downs.

### Eat Me, Drink Me

- Haywagon Inn, High Street, Hartfield, East Sussex. Tel 01892 770252. A good, traditional pub with a garden. Serves lunch till 4 p.m. on Sundays, 3 p.m. on Saturdays.
- The Hatch, Colemans Hatch, nr Forest Row, Hartfield, East Sussex. Tel 01342 822363. Definitely the most popular pub in the area. Serves lunch from 12 p.m. to 2.30 p.m. daily.
- Duddleswell Tea Rooms, Duddleswell, near Fairwarp, Ashdown Forest on the B2026. Tel 01825 712126 or online at

www.duddleswelltearooms. Definitely worth a visit. Open from 10 a.m. to 5 p.m., closed on Wednesdays.
- Wych Cross Garden Centre Tea Shop, Wych Cross Nurseries, Wych Cross, Forest Row, East Grinstead, West Sussex. Tel 01342 822705. Useful if you haven't packed a picnic. Open from 10 a.m. to 4.30 p.m. (4 p.m. in winter) but closed on Sundays.

## Useful Information
- For Ashdown Forest Tourism Association visit www.ashdownforest.com.
- For maps, special events and local information visit Ashdown Forest Visitors Centre, Wych Cross, Forest Row, East Sussex. Tel 01342 823583 or online at www.ashdownforest.org. Open weekends and bank holidays from 11 a.m. to 5 p.m. and weekdays from 2 p.m. to 5 p.m.
- For places to stay contact Wealden Sussex Country on 01323 442667 or online at www.sussexcountry.co.uk/wheretostay.html.
- Tunbridge Wells tourist information is on 01892 515675 or online at www.tunbridgewells.gov.uk/tourism.

## Did you know?
- The house where A.A. Milne lived, Cotchford Farm in Hartfield, was later lived in by Brian Jones, lead guitarist of the Rolling Stones. He drowned in the swimming pool in 1969. The original house has since been demolished.

## Enticing Extras
- Pooh Corner, The High Street, Hartfield, East Sussex. Tel 01892 770456. This was originally the very place where the real Christopher Robin came to buy sweets with his nanny. It now stocks Pooh memorabilia of every kind and has a small tea shop that serves cakes and crumpets.
- The Rainbow Rocking Horses, The Shawe, Millbrook Hill,

Nutley, East Sussex. Tel 01825 712704 or online at www.rainbowrockinghorses.co.uk. They make traditional rocking horses.

- Bramble Corner, The Square, Forest Row, Sussex. Tel 01342 826800 or online at www.bramblecorner.com. This beautiful shop full of old-fashioned toys is really worth a look. Open on Sundays too.

**Rainy Day Options**

- If it really pours down, take refuge on the Bluebell Railway at nearby Horsted Keynes for a steam train ride. Open on weekends and in the summer. Tel 01825 720825 or online at www.bluebell-railway.co.uk.
- Call in at the British Wildlife Centre on the A22. There are keeper talks throughout the day and enclosures where children can see badgers, foxes, red squirrels, otters and birds of prey. Open weekends and school holidays.
  Tel 01342 834658 or online at www.britishwildlifecentre.co.uk.

# 2. High Tower

Leith Hill, Surrey

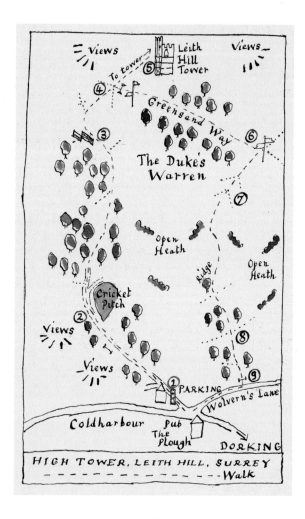

## The Adventure

Climb to the highest point in south-east England 294 m / 965 feet above sea level. Leith Hill in the Surrey Hills, due to its prominence over the surrounding countryside, has been a significant site since the Anglo-Saxon times. In 851AD Ethelwulf, father of Alfred the Great, led and won a great battle against the Danes and saved England for Christianity. Rivers of blood are said to have run down the hillside, with twenty thousand men on each side fighting to their deaths.

The tower sits atop the hill and is 19.5 m / 64 feet tall, a fortified folly in the Gothic style. Richard Hull, who lived in Leith Hill Place, built it in 1765. When he died he was buried under the floor at the bottom of the tower. In the nineteenth century when Caroline Wedgwood, wife of Josiah Wedgwood and sister of Charles Darwin, was living at Leith Hill Place she planted rhododendron bushes on the southern slopes of the hill that still produce a riot of colour in the woods in spring and early summer. Later on the house was lived in by one of Britain's greatest composers, Dr Ralph Vaughan Williams, who started the Leith Hill Music Festival.

On your way through the woods examine all the different variety of trees, bushes and fruits to see how many you can identify. This area is known for whortleberries – see if you can find some – which are similar to the American blueberries. They are found on the plant *Vaccinium myrtillus* and in Scotland they are called blaeberry and in Wales whimberry. If you find some you can use the recipe provided (see page 201) to make a pie.

**Map** Ordnance Survey Explorer Map 146

**Distance** Just over 5 km / 3 miles

**Terrain** Beautiful woodland paths that are well marked with some steep, albeit short, climbs. It's quite a strenuous walk for very little ones.

**What will I need?**
- A picnic
- Binoculars
- A plastic bag for whortleberries
- A sword to re-enact the battle of Leith Hill
- String to make a bow and arrow (see page 24)

**How to get there**
M25 to Junction 8 (could be Junction 9 if coming from west London) and on to the A25 to Dorking. Take the A24 to Horsham and at the roundabout keep going straight on the A24 on to a dual carriageway. At the next roundabout turn right on to the A29 to Ockley. After three quarters of a mile, on the bend, turn right down Henhurst Cross Lane. At the T-junction turn left at the sign saying Leith Hill and Coldharbour. Park outside the Plough Inn if you plan to go there for lunch; otherwise on the right after the letterbox is a small car park.

**What can we listen to on the way?**
- *Andersen's Fairy Tales* (Naxos)
- *Tales from the Norse Legends* (Naxos)

**LAND OF THE SILVER BIRCH**
Land of the silver birch
Home of the beaver
Where still the mighty moose
Wanders at will
Blue lake and rocky shore
I will return once more
Bom, tiddle-i-di, bom, tiddle-i-di,
Bom, tiddle-i-di,
Bom.

- *Fairy Tales* by Terry Jones (Orion)
- *Famous Composers 2* including Vaughan Williams (Naxos)

## Walk the Walk

**1** Walk up the track between the telephone box and letterbox marked public byway. It soon splits. Take the right path, signed Tower and cricket ground, going up a fairly steep hill surrounded by birch, pines and holly. Pass a bench with great views of the Downs below.

**2** As the track levels out you come to Coldharbour Common and cricket ground with stunning views. Do stop to take a look. Pass the pitch, leaving it to your right, and take the wide track on the left. Keep going along this gorse and bracken edged byway ignoring any turns to the left or the right.

**3** Stay on this byway until the track starts to bend downhill. You come to a junction with a path coming from the left with a wooden fence near by. Take the first right fork down the hill.

**4** At the bottom is a crossroads of five paths. Turn left up the hill past the National Trust sign to Leith Hill Tower. This is a steep climb but a short one.

**5** Once you've got your breath back, climb the tower to get the best views: you are now 3113 m / 1029 feet above sea level. Through the telescope you can see panoramic views of the south coast and the English Channel to the south and St Paul's Cathedral to the north.

## MAKE A BOW AND ARROW

Cut a length of hazel or young, flexible wood, about three quarters of the height of your budding knight. Cut a small notch at either end to hold the string and stop it from slipping. Tie a length of string from the top to the bottom and tighten.

Cut smaller, straight sticks for arrows. Peel off the bark to make them stand out. They don't need arrow heads and are safer without them. They will fire dramatic distances and create hours of entertainment for children of all ages. Prepare to make plenty of arrows to replace the lost ones.

Hazel

Take a break at the bottom of the tower: play out some battles; play 40/40. Look out for the blackberry bushes behind the tower. Have your picnic and a hot cup of tea at the tea room in the tower.

After lunch head back down the hill the way you came up until you get back to the five-way crossroads. At this point, turn left along a public bridleway (the Greensand Way) going gently downhill through a wooded valley full of silver birch trees. Did you know that the bark of a silver birch peels off fairly easily and can be used for writing on? Try it as long as you are careful not to damage the tree.

**6** At the well-marked four-way crossroads with a fingerpost and a stone saying E1915, turn right along a muddy track. You are no longer on the Greensand Way but still on a bridleway. Cross the little brook heading in to Duke's Warren – you will see a National Trust signpost.

**7** The path immediately splits three ways – take the main path straight ahead going uphill. At the next three-way split stay on the middle path. You get a great view of the tower on your right. Carry on going straight on the main track. You are now on top of a ridge, with views in both directions, in an area of open ground. You might see some foxgloves. Keep to this main track, walking straight on

where a bridleway crosses the path.

**8** At the second crossroads of paths go straight on. Follow along the ridge heading downhill through the pine trees gathering pine cones on the way. The path becomes an ancient lane banked by beech trees that were planted as boundary banks.

**9** Walk through the wooden barrier and turn right on to the byway downhill along Wolvern's Lane, a ten to fifteen minute walk back to the car.

### Eat Me, Drink Me

- The Plough Inn, Coldharbour, nr Dorking, Surrey.
  Tel 01306 711793 or online at www.theploughinn.com.
  A seventeenth-century coaching inn with accommodation, delicious home cooked food, and beers including Tickety Boo, Tallywhacker and Crooked Farrow from the Leith Hill Brewery.
- The tea room in Leith Hill Tower sells homemade cakes, snacks and simple food. Tel 01306 711777. Opening hours vary.
- Stephen Langton Inn, Friday Street, Abinger Common, Dorking, Surrey. Tel 01306 730775. A nearby pub in a beautiful location. Friday Street is a small hamlet near Abinger Common.

## CREATE A MINIATURE CASTLE

Gather moss and stones and build a motte and bailey castle. Pile the mud to make mounds and ditches. Make a tiny fence, ramparts and a miniature drawbridge out of sticks.

### Useful Information

- Leith Hill Tower is open from the end of March to the end of October, Friday, Saturday and Sunday from 10 a.m. to 5 p.m. In the winter, it is open Saturday and Sunday only from 10 a.m. to 3.30 p.m. Open all bank holidays except Christmas Day. Tel 01306 712434 for opening hours, or visit www.nationaltrust.org.uk.
- For information about further attractions, walks and accommodation in the area visit www.surreyhills.org.
- Surrey Wildlife Trust organise nature events and activities for families. Find out what's on at www.surreywildlifetrust.org.uk.

### Did you know?

- During World War I the juice of whortleberries was used to dye army uniforms.
- Leith Hill has been a favourite picnic site since Victorian times.

### Enticing Extras

- Etherley Farm at the foot of the hill has a shop selling oven-ready geese, turkey, and duck, free-range eggs and chutneys. You can also camp at the farm all year round. Tel 01306 621423.

### Rainy Day Options

- Visit Polesden Lacey, Great Bookham, Dorking, Surrey. Tel 01372 452048 or online at www.nationaltrust.org.uk. The house is closed from November to just before Easter. The gardens and grounds are open all week. Entry fee charged.

# 3. Beach Ramble

Mersea Island, Blackwater Estuary, Essex

**The Adventure**

This wild stretch of seaside has all you want from a beach, with fabulous shells, fossils in the cliff face, wading birds and geese colonies, sand to build castles and open sea. Mersea is a real island that is cut off from the mainland when the tide is in. Drive across the Strood, a causeway, to get there, but beware when the tides are highest as you can be marooned.

The soft cliff above the beach is a palaeontologist's dream. Under the 300, 000 year old Pleistocene deposits are the fossilised bones of the animals who once roamed over this Essex land. The fossils of hippo, bear, monkey, wolf and straight-tusked elephants have all been found.

Colonies of sand martins have made their home in the sea-cliffs, digging holes in the soft earth to make their nests, raising their young here before they set off for Africa for the winter. On the beach, there are nationally important numbers of redshank, grey

cormorant

plover, comorant and ringed plover. Look out for shelduck, avocets, curlew and oystercatchers, too. Every time the tide goes out, a new, rich food supply is revealed. Across the other side of the sea wall are the feeding plains for the 3,000 brent geese that fly here in January to winter. This mixed habitat, with arable fields to one side, and the salt marshes and mudflats to the other, is perfect for attracting huge numbers of birds to one small area.

In the summer, the shore is littered with the remains of the harmless moon jellyfish and small crabs. Deep banks of shells provide rich pickings for beachcombers and treasure seekers. Make sandcastles, string shells together to make necklaces, dig in the mud and find mud worms.

curlew

Take a five minute ferry ride over the waters to the seaside town of Brightlingsea for fish and chips and a wander past the brightly painted beach huts. After your walk drive into the town of West Mersea on the other side of the island. After all that sea air, you might have built up an appetite for some seafood. Head for the seafront and try one of the oyster sheds selling the freshest seafood you'll ever taste. This is Whitstable before the crowds.

**Map** Ordnance Survey Explorer Map 184

**Distance** 2 km / 1.2 miles. You can walk all the way round the island which has a 9 mile circumference.

**Terrain** Beach, sea, sand. When not on the beach, it is a flat walk along the sea wall.

**What will I need?**
• Bucket and spade

- A container for shells
- Crabbing kit
- Binoculars
- A bird spotter's log book to write down what you've seen
- A bottle, paper and pen to send a message out to sea
- Swimming costumes for the brave
- Hats on a hot day as there is little shade
- Drinks and a light picnic for the beach, leaving room for fresh prawns and oysters later
- If you like to fish, bring a line, bait and sinkers, as the waters opposite Brightlingsea are deep and good for fishing.

knotted cockle

## How to get there

Take the A12 to Junction 18, then the A414 towards Maldon. Meander along the B1026 towards Tolleshunt D'Arcy and then cut through to the B1025, following signs to Mersea Island. Cudmore Grove beach is at the east end of the island, turning left after the causeway. It is clearly signposted as Cudmore Grove Country Park at the end of Bromans Lane where there is a car park. The town, and the oyster shacks, are on the other side of the island, to the west.

## What can we listen to on the way?

- Cliff Richard's 'We're all going on a summer holiday'
- Beach Boys *Greatest Hits*
- *Five Children and It* by E. Nesbit (Naxos)
- *The Treasure Seekers* by E. Nesbit (Naxos)
- *Three Little Pirates by* Georgie Adams (Orion)

## Walk the Walk

**1** Cut through the hedge line of the car park and turn right, following the hedgerow and picnic tables towards the woods.

After a bench dedicated to Doris Lillian Day, take the path to the left and scramble down to the beach below.

**2** When the tide is out, the sand becomes mudflats, stretching into the distance. Stay a while here, making sandcastles, collecting shells and gathering driftwood. The broken concrete slabs across the sand are the remains of gun emplacements from World War II.

**3** Head left along the beach. Before long, there is a path to your left taking you back through the field to the car park. Ignore this and carry straight on along the sea's edge. Across the inlet is the seaside town of Brightlingsea and its colourful beach huts. It has a stretch of beach, fish and chips and a Martello tower (see page 34). You can take a ferry across. From Easter to October, call 01206 302200 and the ferry will come and pick you up. In summer months and on bank holidays, the ferry runs all day so there is no need to call. It takes nine minutes to get across and they will bring you back again by arrangement. Adults are £1 each way, children and dogs 50p. Wait at the sign on the end of the island, directly opposite the town.

## SHELLS TO LOOK OUT FOR

Pink scallop

Weathervane scallop

Blue mussel

Common limpet

Common edible cockle

Mermaid's purse

Common piddock

Grooved razor clam

Common whelk

Striped Venus

Noah's Ark

Winkle

## BEACH COMBING

Set off across the beach looking for whelks eggs, mermaid's purse, crabs, razor shells, oyster shells, cockle shells, mussels, star fish, sea urchin, seaweed, bird feathers, scallop shells, jellyfish (don't touch), cuttlefish bones and driftwood. Ask children to bring their finds back to one spot for everyone to see what they've found. String hagstones and shells together to make decorations, mobiles or jewellery. Find large pebbles and paint them. When the tide is out, dig in the mudflats: discover ragworms, molluscs and mud beetles. Take an old bottle, a piece of paper and a pen to write a message. Seal it tight and throw it ceremoniously out to sea.

Variegated scallop

4 As the island curves round, the Blackwater–Colne estuary is very deep and a good place to stop for a bit of fishing. Look out for the Martello tower across the sea. When you are opposite, there will be an 8 knots sign behind you on the shore. This is also the foot ferry landing point.

5 Walk to the sign and head back on a path that runs parallel to and above the beach. The path goes over a small concrete bridge (which can be flooded at high tide) and up some steps to a high sea wall. Turn left and walk along it if you want to go straight back to the car; if not turn right and walk along the sea wall to extend the walk as far as you like, eventually retracing your steps back. The very energetic can walk around the entire island on this sea wall footpath. It takes a good four hours and is very exposed so make sure you have the Ordnance Survey map and are well protected from the weather.

6 Heading home, follow the sea wall back or drop down to the grassy path below to get a good look at the birds as they feed on the grassy flood plains.

Walk through the gate and turn right across the open field up to the car park, passing a wartime pillbox, and back to your car.

**Eat Me, Drink Me**

- In the summer there is usually an ice cream van in the car park at Cudmore Grove.
- Buy fish and chips from the sea front at Brightlingsea if you take the ferry across.
- Drive to West Mersea and the town. Follow the road along the sea front until you come to the boat harbour and the Company Shed. It is really a fishmonger with a café on the side, but has become one of the most sought-after places to eat on the east coast. Squeeze along plain tables and benches, bring your own bread and wine and tuck in to the best, freshest and highest quality seafood. Open from 9 a.m. to 5 p.m. Last orders to eat in at 4 p.m. Closed on Mondays.

common edible cockle

The Company Shed, 129 Coast Road, West Mersea, Essex. Tel 01206 382700. Specialises in flat oysters (September to April), lobster, crabs, prawns, cockles, herrings, smoked mackerel and Norfolk green-lipped mussels.

Blue Mussel

- Try the wonderful West Mersea Oyster Bar on the same road: The Oyster Sheds, Coast Road, West Mersea, Essex. Tel 01206 381600. Serves West Mersea rock oysters and Colchester native oysters, fish and chips, mussels, crab, salmon and prawns, wine and beer.

**Useful Information**
- Check the tide tables before you go at www.mersea-island.com as The Strood (the causeway) can be under water and impassable for cars with low clearance at certain times of day.
- For places to stay visit www.mersea-island.com.

**Did you know?**
- Two thousand years ago, the Romans made salt here. The nearby village of Maldon is still famous for its high-quality salt.
- Martello towers are fortifications built by the British Army for coastal defence in the nineteenth century. They were built all over the British Empire from Ireland to Canada.

**Rainy Day Options**
- The Mersea Island Museum. Tel 01206 385191 or online at www.merseamuseum.org.uk. An independent museum in West Mersea representing the traditional local activities of fishing, oystering, wildfowling and boat building. Open May to September, 2 p.m. to 5 p.m. Wednesday to Sunday and bank holidays.

# 4. Wind in the Willows

Henley-on-Thames, Oxfordshire

**The Adventure**

This trip starts in the village of Remenham and takes us along the banks of the River Thames. Hopefully, like Mole, you will become 'intoxicated with the sparkle, the ripple, the scent, and the sounds and the sunlight' of it all. Things to do along the way include: looking for a badgers' sett (look on the map for some clues as to where you might find one); watching the lock-keeper at work; keeping an eye out for interesting birds – we saw a magnificent heron at the weir – and seeing if you can identify the many different types of boats including a sailing boat, a punt, a houseboat and a 'brand new wager boat' just like the ones fickle Mr Toad had crazes for. We also saw some beautiful dragonflies when we were there.

## Mole's first sight of the River Thames
from *The Wind in the Willows* by Kenneth Grahame

Never in his life had he seen a river before — this sleek, sinuous, full-bodied animal, chasing and chuckling, gripping things with a gurgle and leaving them with a laugh, to fling itself on fresh playmates that shook themselves free, and were caught and held again. All was a-shake and a-shiver — glints and gleams and sparkles, rustle and swirl, chatter and bubble. The Mole was bewitched, entranced, fascinated. By the side of the river he trotted as one trots, when very small, by the side of a man who holds one spell-bound by exciting stories; and when tired at last, he sat on the bank, while the river still chattered on to him, a babbling procession of the best stories in the world, sent from the heart of the earth to be told at last to the insatiable sea.

**Map** Ordnance Survey Explorer Map 171

**Distance** 5 km / 3 miles

**Terrain** Very easy flat walk, mostly along well-maintained paths

**What will I need?**
- Take a picnic to enjoy on the banks of the river as there is so much action to watch on the water.
- Be inspired by Rat's picnic fare for his trip down the river with Mole: 'coldtonguecoldhamcoldbeefpickledgherkinssaladfrenchrollscressand-widgespottedmeatgingerberlemonade-sodawater'
- A copy of *The Wind in the Willows* by Kenneth Grahame, illustrated by E.H. Shepard

Toad

## How to get there

Take the M40 to Junction 4. Turn left on to the A404, direction Marlow. Then take the A4130 to Henley-on-Thames. Before the steep hill down to Henley you will see a turning on your right to Aston Town and shortly afterwards one to Remenham Church. Take this and drive all the way to the church where you should park.

## What can we listen to on the way?

• *The Wind in the Willows* by Kenneth Grahame, read by Alan Bennett (BBC)

## Walk the Walk

1 Face the church and walk up the lane on the right leaving the church to your left. Keep going until you reach a fork in the road and turn right on to Church Lane. Walk all the way up the hill.

2 At the first footpath sign, turn left and walk across the middle of an open field following the path. Keep going straight as the path narrows, ignoring what looks like a path to the right.

There is a 'no public access' notice on a tree, making it obvious which path to follow.

Water Shrew

3 Just before reaching a gate, head left and follow the path down. It is here you want to be looking out for badger setts and paw prints. Badgers are part of the weasel family and often build their setts in sloping sandy soils in woodland and near pastureland. They mainly like to eat earthworms and are very shy so if you want to see one you will have to stand very still and try and keep out of the badger's eye line.

As you come to the lane, climb over the stile and turn right. This is Aston village and there is a good pub here, the Flower Pot, that is worth a stop either for food or just a drink. To find the pub you need to walk just beyond the next footpath turning.

4 Turn left before the pub, following the public footpath sign. Walk along the gravel path as it bends through the field. You are now heading for the river.

5 Just before you get to the river, you will pass a small but interesting bog. Take a look in here as it's the perfect habitat for frogs, toads and water rats. There are also small streams, perfect for little creatures. Walk on a little and you will see the river ahead of you. Follow the Thames Path going left. Hambledon Lock and the weir are just ahead. Do take the time to walk across the lock and half way over the weir bridge as you might see some fantastic birds. The roar of the water is exhilarating too.

6 Retrace your steps back to the Thames Path and pick up the path again heading towards Henley. A little further on you will see a grand white house on the opposite bank that we like to think of as Toad Hall. Somewhere along here is the best place to picnic.

7 Keep going and as you approach Temple Island – the official

starting place of the Henley Royal Regatta boat course – look down the river to get a view of Henley and the church.

Just after this point there is a metal fence alongside the path. Here you will find a footpath sign sending you left through a gate away from the river. Before you turn off though, just a little bit further along the Thames Path, there is often an ice cream van. The children will undoubtedly spot it a mile off if it's there.

**8** Go through the kissing gate and follow the path back to the church and your car.

## COLLECTIVE NOUNS OF ANIMALS AND BIRDS

A pack of wolves

A skulk of foxes

A harras of horses

A trip of goats

A murder of crows

A knot of toads

A colony of bats

A sloth of bears

An army of caterpillars

A labour of moles

A harvest of mice

A gaggle of geese

A parliament of owls

A colony of beavers

A flock of birds

A rabble of butterflies

A brood of chicks

A sounder of wild boars

A clamour of rooks

A clutter of spiders

A chattering of starlings

A pack of weasels

A business of ferrets

A cloud of flies

A flight of herons

A tiding of magpies

A watch of nightingales

A bevy of otters

A sting of ponies

A hive of oysters

An unkindness of ravens

Heron

**Eat Me, Drink Me**
- The Flower Pot Hotel, Aston, Berkshire. Tel 01491 574721. This is a good pub with a children's menu which serves food seven days a week from 12 p.m. to 2 p.m. and from 6.30 p.m. in the evening. Buggies are not allowed in the dining room but there is a beer garden.
- Henley is full of places to eat.

**Useful Information**
- Hobbs of Henley rent out all different sizes of rowing boats and motor launches, and also provide river trips or will do private charters. Tel 01491 572035 or online at www.hobbs-of-henley.com.
- For local information on accommodation and things to visit go to www.visithenley-on-thames.com.

**Did you know?**
- The source of the River Thames is in Gloucestershire and its course runs 180 miles all the way from here to the Thames Barrier in London.

**Rainy Day Options**
- The River and Rowing Museum, Mill Meadows, Henley-on-Thames. Tel 01491 415600 or online at www.rrm.co.uk. This has a fantastic collection of river and rowing boats as well as a permanent exhibition of *Wind in the Willows*. There is also a shop and café.
- For information about badgers contact the Badger Trust on 0207 228 6444 or online at www.nfbg.org.uk.

badger

# 5. Dick Turpin: Hideouts and Highwaymen

Epping Forest, Loughton, Essex

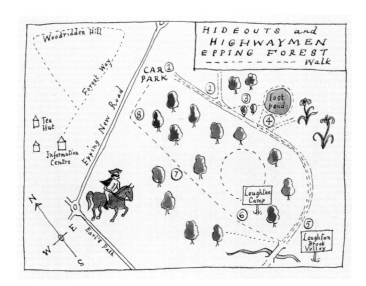

**The Adventure**

This is a fantastic expedition to the ancient Epping Forest, declared by Queen Victoria in 1821 as 'the people's forest'. It is a great place to make camp and play ambush games just like the legendary highwayman Dick Turpin might have done in his day. It is said that Turpin used to stash his loot and hide out at Loughton Camp, an Iron Age fort, which you will visit on this trip. Explore the forest to find the Lost Pond and take the opportunity to do some fishing (providing you have the right licence – see page 47 for details) or build a twig house, whittle sticks and climb trees. Practising orienteering would be a valuable exercise here too as it's easy to get lost in a forest. Also keep your eyes open as Epping is a Site of Special Scientific Interest and many rare plants and animal species can be found here. You might even see deer, as about five hundred roam in the forest and deer sanctuary.

Fallow deer

**Map** Ordnance Survey Explorer Map 174

**Distance** 3 km / 1.8 miles

**Terrain** Well-maintained gravel or sand paths and woodland tracks. Gentle incline. Can be muddy.

**What will I need?**
- A picnic – there is no obvious place to buy food en route and nowhere once you are parked up at the forest. If you visit the information centre a car ride away there is a tea hut sited across the road that sells the basics.
- A compass. It is easy to get disorientated in a forest even though you are only a mile away from the road at any point.
- A penknife for whittling sticks or making a fishing rod
- Bread to feed the mandarin ducks at the Lost Pond
- Dressing up sword and highwayman's cloak
- A tent. There is a campsite at Debden where you can have real camp fires.

**How to get there**
Take the M11 for five minutes to Junction 5. Turn off and take the A1168 towards Loughton. Drive through a series of mini roundabouts after which you turn right on to the A121 towards Epping and Waltham Abbey. Drive up Goldings Hill for a short distance, and into Epping Forest. At the roundabout, turn left on to to the A104, signposted Epping Forest Centre. Drive past a car

park on the right and park in the first car park on the left.

## What can we listen to on the way?
- *Stig of the Dump* by Clive King (Penguin)
- *The Best of Our Island Story* (Naxos)

## Walk the Walk
1 Head out of the car park through the metal gate. Walk along the sandy bridleway leaving the road behind you. You are entering London's largest public open space. It is one of the last parts of the great oak forest that surrounded London until medieval times. After 500 m / 550 yards this path joins another path. Veer right.
2 Immediately opposite you will see a small footpath leading into Monk Wood. You are going a short distance into the wood to discover the Lost Pond. Follow the path and keep walking straight ahead. You soon hit another path heading left. Go with it.
3 Shortly you will arrive at the Lost Pond (Black Weir Pond) that was created in 1895 from the remains of a gravel pit where you can try your hand at fishing (provided you have the correct permits). See if you can find a fallen log with iron rungs: this is all that remains of a lookout post from World War II. If you hunt carefully round the southern side of the pond you should find a very large beech tree that is reputed to be over a thousand years old. It's fun to play at the pond or even have lunch here, but the main part of the walk is yet to come.
4 Leave on the path you entered by which is in the south-west corner of the pond. But this time, keep walking straight on, don't veer right, leaving the wood a different way. Get out your compass and continue in a south-westerly direction. You will soon come out on to the same maintained gravel track you were on before you entered the wood, just in a different place.
5 Turn left here and walk down the hill to the bottom. Just before you reach a little stream, a bridge and a

signpost saying Loughton Brook Valley, you will see two small paths off to the right almost next-door to each other. Take the first one. This path heads off in a north-westerly direction, climbing upwards, and becomes better defined as you walk along it.

**6** As the path climbs up in to the woods you should see a sign ahead for Loughton Camp. This was built circa 500BC and was used as animal folds in times of attack from other tribes, or as lookout posts and boundary markers between neighbouring tribes, the

## TRACKING AND TRAIL FINDING

A great way to keep the adventure going is to get the children involved in a tracking expedition. Send a party of native trackers ahead of the main group to leave a trail of clues for them to follow.

Use simple arrows made of sticks or stones on the pathways to show the way. Mark paths with a cross if they are not the right way. Tie branches and leaves together to block a turning. Drop trails of pebbles, like Hansel and Gretel.

Decide which symbols you are going to use before you set off. Create your own secret set of symbols and signs if you wish.

THIS WAY
ARROW

THIS WAY
POINTER

DO NOT GO THIS
WAY
STONES

THE RIGHT WAY
STONES

TURN RIGHT

DO NOT GO THIS
WAY

GONE HOME

GONE HOME

Trinovantes and the Catevellauni. This camp was still being used in Roman times. Keep your eyes on the forest floor as worked flints can occasionally be found. Sit down, set up camp and make lunch.

**7** When you are ready to head home, find the path you entered the camp by. If you are disorientated make your way back to the signpost you walked past on the way in. Continue on this well-defined path out of the woods with Loughton Camp to your right. The ground by the path slopes away to the left and the walls of the camp, on your right, get higher as you walk along.

**8** Keep heading out on the same path in a straight line. Once you can see the road ahead turn right, taking a path that is parallel to the road. You will soon be back at your car.

### Eat Me, Drink Me

- The forest area has little in the way of good food. There is a hut opposite the visitor information centre (see page 46 for details) that sells sandwiches, crisps and drinks.

- Loughton has dozens of restaurants, including Pizza Express, 281–283 High Road, tel 0208 508 3303, Chez Gérard,

### CAMOUFLAGE

The woods are the perfect place for playing ambush and camouflage games. Take along some face paints and paint their faces green and brown to hide in the bushes or just smear with mud. See how well they can hide themselves in a small area. Use fallen leaves and branches to cover their bodies. Challenge them to get 'home' without being spotted.

275–277 High Road, tel 0208 508 5399, and the Loch Fyne Restaurant, 280–282 High Road, tel 0208 532 5140.

## Useful Information

- Epping Forest Visitor Centre, High Beach, Loughton, Essex. Tel 0208 508 0028 or online at www.cityoflondon.gov.uk. Interesting exhibits, leaflets and things for the children. Open from 1st April to 31st October weekdays and Saturdays from 10 a.m. to 5 p.m. Sundays and bank holidays 11 a.m. to 5 p.m. Open from 1st November to 31st March weekdays and Saturdays 10 a.m. to 4 p.m. Sundays and bank holidays 11a.m. to dusk.
- Debden Campsite, Debden House, Debden Green, Loughton, Essex. Tel 0208 508 3008 or online at www.debdenhouse.com. Open from beginning of May to end of September annually, this 50 acre campsite comprises seven camp fields: three for ordinary camping with electricity; three (two of which are for group bookings only) with fire pits for real campfires and barbecuing (these sites have to be pre-booked and require driver's licence i.d. on arrival) and one field that has a permanent marquee erected that is available for hire. Adults are £7 per person per night, children under 15, £3.50. There are toilet facilities, showers, a laundry, and sinks with running water. Dogs on a leash are permitted, £1.

- For information on open spaces in London visit www.cityoflondon.gov.uk/openspaces.
- Fishing licences must be obtained for anyone over the age of 12. Buy one online from www.environment-agency.gov.uk/fish.

## Did you know?

- Dick Turpin is a legendary eighteenth-century English rogue and the most famous historical highwayman. In life Richard Turpin was a bad man who went from deer stealing to burglary, to highway robbery and even murder, for which he was executed in 1739. Posthumously he became the subject of legend, romanticised in ballads and popular theatre of the eighteenth and nineteenth century, and later in film and television of the twentieth century, as the dashing and heroic highwayman.

## Rainy Day Options

- Visit Waltham Abbey, one of Britain's finest Norman buildings where King Harold was buried after the Battle of Hastings. For information visit www.walthamabbeychurch.co.uk.
- Epping Forest Museum, 39–41 Sun Street, Waltham Abbey. Tel 01992 716882 or online at www.eppingforestdc.gov.uk. Includes archaeological finds of prehistoric tools found at Loughton Camp.
- Queen Elizabeth's Hunting Lodge, originally known as the Great Standing, Rangers Road (B1081), Chingford. Tel 0208 529 6681 or online at www.cityoflondon.gov.uk. Built for King Henry VIII in 1543, it was used as a grandstand to watch the hunting of deer, or possibly from which to shoot deer with crossbows. It is the only remaining timber-framed standing in England, possibly in Europe, and is an excellent example of Tudor carpentry. Children can try on the dressing-up clothes, or have a go at brass rubbing.

Turkey Oak

# 6. Changing the Guard at Buckingham Palace

The Mall, London

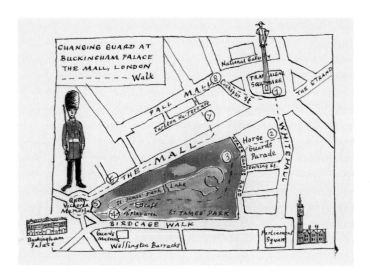

## The Adventure

Step into A.A. Milne's poem about Christopher Robin and Alice going to Buckingham Palace to see the Changing of the Guard: get close up to the soldiers; try to make the guardsmen blink; follow the parade and chase the band to St James's Palace. Pretend to be a real tourist in London and take photographs of all the famous landmarks you'll see as well as the soldiers, and paste them into a scrapbook as a memory of the day. Have a photograph taken next to a guardsman – there's one standing all on his own if you go to St James's Palace, walk past the courtyard and turn left around the corner (into Pall Mall.)

There are several different changes of the Guard going on

simultaneously, at Horse Guards Parade, St James's Palace, Wellington Barracks and Buckingham Palace. This route avoids the crowds and shows you a lot of action. Check details of the parade before you leave home on the website (see page 53). If it is very wet the Changing of the Guard does not take place.

They're changing guard at Buckingham Palace –

Christopher Robin went down with Alice.

Alice is marrying one of the guard.

'A soldier's life is terrible hard' says Alice

A.A. Milne

**Map** *London A–Z*

**Distance** Less than 2 km / 1.2 miles

**Terrain** London streets and St James's Park

**What will I need?**
- A copy of A.A. Milne's *When We Were Very Young*
- A watch (timing is everything on this walk)
- A camera – pretend to be a tourist: take pictures of all the interesting buildings, monuments and statues you walk past and make a scrapbook of your day when you get home.
- A Guard's uniform from the dressing-up box complete with busby – maybe leave the gun at home

**How to get there**
There are several stations close to Trafalgar Square, including Charing Cross and Leicester Square. For information call Transport for London on 0207 222 1234 or vist www.tfl.gov.uk.

**Walk the Walk**
**1** Start at Trafalgar Square. A great place to left off steam, admire the lions, splash in the fountains. Crane your neck to look at

Nelson on top of his column.

**2** With the National Gallery behind you cross on to Whitehall and walk down here on the right-hand pavement. Take a right between the two guarding horses and walk under the archway into Horse Guards Parade. This is the best place to get close to the horses. Get here a bit before 11 a.m. so you can take a close look at the soldiers doing their job: the sentries are on horseback until 4 p.m. The Changing of the Guard here starts at 11 a.m. (10 a.m. on Sundays). Once the new Guard has arrived, on horseback from Knightsbridge, stay here for about ten minutes. Have a good look at the horses, study the soldiers' uniforms and see if you can identify which regiment they are from (see Useful Information page 53). The Household Division is made up of seven regiments: two Household Cavalry regiments – the Life Guards and the Blues and Royals; and five regiments of Foot Guards – the Grenadier Guards, the Coldstream Guards, the Scots Guards, the Irish Guards and the Welsh Guards. In August

### THE GRAND OLD DUKE OF YORK

The grand old Duke of York,
He had ten thousand men.
He marched them up to the top of the hill
And he marched them down again.

And when they were up, they were up;
And when they were down, they were down.
But when they were only halfway up,
They were neither up nor down!

Sing it straight, sing it in a round, then try it missing out the words up, then down, then both and see who can do it!

other regiments often guard the Queen.

**3** Cross over Horse Guards into St James's Park. Turn left and then right down the path heading to Buckingham Palace. Keep going all the way to the end and near a small play park and sandwich kiosk leave the park and cross over to Wellington Barracks.

**4** Here the foot soldiers are preparing to change the Guard and march to the Palace. There are no horses but they do have a band that you will have been able to hear whilst walking through the park. The crowds don't gather here in the same way they do outside the Palace so it's easy to see what's going on. These soldiers march to the Palace at about 11.30 a.m. Just before they are due to leave, run and get a pitch on the pavement on the way to the Palace. This way you will get a fantastic view of the soldiers and the band marching along.

**5** It is really too crowded to see what is going on at the Palace so take this opportunity to go back into the park and have a quick rest and a play. In 1603 the park was laid out with a menagerie for James I and in 1667 exotic birds were introduced, including

the pelicans. Besides this there are eiders, cormorants, grey herons, teal and grebe as well as the more usual moorhens, coots and geese. Tawny owls nest in the trees here in spring and early summer. There are swings and picnic tables in this part of the park, as well as children-only lavatories.

**6** Come out of the park on to the Mall at about 12.05 p.m., cross to the other side and line up along the pavement's edge. From here you will be in the best position to follow the outgoing Guard from Buckingham Palace who come past at 12.15 p.m. heading back to St James's Palace. Have fun marching along with the band, down the Mall and left toward St James's Palace. This is a real highlight as you are right alongside the marching soldiers.

**7** Head back down the tree-lined Mall, turning left up the steps just before the ICA towards the statue of Frederick, Duke of York, Commander of the British Army and the Grand Old Duke of York. Chant the rhyme as you climb the steps.

**8** Make your way back to the top of Trafalgar Square by turning right on to Pall Mall, crossing over the zebra crossing in front of you.

**Eat Me, Drink Me**

• Inn in the Park, St James's Park. Tel 0207 451 9999. The restaurant offers a children's menu, though at £7.50 or £9.50 for

a child's portion, you may be better off having a sandwich or snack from their self-service menu.
• National Gallery Dining Room in the Sainsbury wing. Afternoon tea from 3 p.m. or light meals: smoked mackerel on toast, soups and a children's menu.

**Useful Information**
• For up-to-date information about the Changing the Guard schedule visit www.changing-the-guard.com. Click on regiments for information about Guards regiments and their uniforms.
• For information on the Household Cavalry visit www.householdcavalry.co.uk.
• The pelicans in the park are fed at 2.30 p.m.
• You can take a tour of Duck Island. For more information visit www.royalparks.com.

**Did you know?**
• The responsibility of guarding the Sovereign by the Household Troops (as they were known at the time) dates back to the reign of Henry VII (1485–1509).

**Rainy Day Options**
• The Guards Museum, Wellington Barracks, Birdcage Walk, London, where you can try on a bearskin. For information visit www.theguardsmuseum.com.
• The State Rooms at Buckingham Palace are open to visitors during the summer season. See work by Rembrandt, Reubens, Vermeer, Poussin, Canaletto and Claude. One of the best bits is walking out of the back entrance of the Palace through the garden. Ticket office and visitor entrance open from 9.15 a.m. to 5 p.m. For more information visit www.royal.gov.uk.

Coot.

# 7. chitty chitty Bang Bang

Turville, The Chilterns, Buckinghamshire

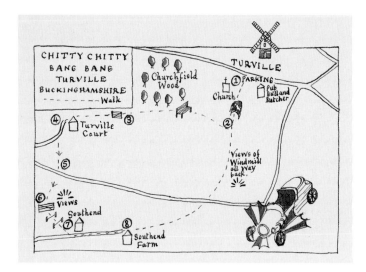

**The Adventure**

This is the place where they filmed the children's classic *Chitty Chitty Bang Bang*, complete with the windmill on the hill where Caractacus, Jemima, Jeremy and Grandpa Potts lived. The windmill is on the hill above the village and through a stretch of rolling green countryside less than forty-five minutes from West London.

Turville itself is a picture postcard village with a fabulous pub. It has been used for filming many times, including the Vicar of Dibley and Inspector Morse. Create an adventure, escaping to the top of the hill opposite the windmill. The paths take you through organic farmland owned by Turville Court Farm. There are wild flowers in abundance and poppies in the fields.

Sing the songs, tell stories of pirates, spies, castles and child catchers. Keep on the look out for the Vulgarian Baron Bombast and his child-hating wife. Watch out for flying cars.

Great Spotted Woodpecker

**Map** Ordnance Survey Explorer Map 171

**Distance** 4 km / 2.5 miles

**Terrain** Rolling fields, clear paths, one mild uphill at the start of the walk. The last stretch is gently downhill all the way.

**What will I need?**
- The words to all the songs from the movie (see page 58)
- A bag of toot sweets
- Fudge
- Binoculars for bird watching, looking out for pirates and to see the windmill in close up

**How to get there**
Take the M40 out of London and come off at Junction 5. Turn left off the motorway towards Ibstone. Soon after Ibstone village is the County primary school. Turn right here, on a narrow lane down to Turville. Take the signposted left into the village. Park on the village green, between the church and the pub.

**What can we listen to on the way?**
The *Chitty Chitty Bang Bang* soundtrack. There are two CDs available. The one published by Pickwick is the original motion picture soundtrack with Dick van Dyke and Sally Ann Howes. The other is the original cast of the London stage show, published by Mr Bang Bang.

## Walk the Walk

1 Walk past the telephone box, towards the church, and take the left turning up the lane, past Sleepy Cottage and the village nursery school. The tarmac lane soon becomes a footpath shaded by trees.

2 Go through the gate at the open field and carry straight on for 90 m / 100 yards, before turning right through a wooden gate in the hedgerow. Follow a clear path up the hill through the open field, passing a conveniently placed resting bench at the top.

3 Look back at the view of the windmill behind you. Look out, too, for pairs of circling red kites as we are close to the area where these elegant birds were recently reintroduced to Britain. Head on to the gate at the very top. Walk straight on through the gate and along the hedgerow.

4 At the tarmac lane, follow the road left, past the big gates of Turville Court (the place to sing POSH). Then turn immediately left on to the marked footpath and into a field. Walk down, over the stile, heading straight through the field, steeply down to the bottom of the hill.

5 Cross over the lane and climb the stile opposite into the next field.

**MAKE A CATAPULT TO DEFEND YOURSELF AGAINST THE WICKED BARON AND BARONESS BOMBURST OR VULGARIA'S EVIL CHILDSNATCHER**

Find a stick with a y-shaped fork. Shorten the top branches of the y to about 8 cm / 3 inches and the handle to a manageable size for small hands. About 3 cm / 1 inch down, cut a notch in the bark and tie a length of rubber (a thick rubber band will work well) to both sides of the y. Give yourself just enough length to pull back slightly. Find some ammunition and fire, well away from others.

**6** Head across this field in a perfectly straight line up to a five bar gate at the top. Climb over two stiles into an arable field, looking out for the views of the windmill to your left.

**7** Halfway through this field, there is a fingerpost in the hedgerow pointing left. Bear left here, on a well-defined path cut through the wheat crop, towards some cottages.

**8** Turn left on to a tarmac lane and past Southend Farm. You are now on the Chiltern Way, a well-marked footpath that takes you in a more or less straight line, downhill all the way back to Turville. Aim for the windmill directly ahead of you.

Once back in the village, it is worth popping up to the windmill to get a closer look, but it is a very steep climb. Bear in mind that it is on private land, on the other side of the fence. You get the best view of the windmill from the walk. But the views of the valley from the hillside are well worth the scramble.

**Eat Me, Drink Me**
• The Bull and Butcher Pub, Turville, Henley-on-Thames.
Tel 01491 638283 or online at www.thebullandbutcher.com.
Lunch is served on Sundays and bank holidays from 12 p.m. to 4 p.m. and from 12 p.m. to 2.30 p.m. the rest of the week.

Just what you want from a pub. Good food as well as a children's menu that serves Chitty Chitty Bangers and chips, and a beer garden. Ales from the Wychwood Brewery. Very busy so worth booking.

## Useful Information
- For information about the Chiltern hills and events in the area, contact The Chilterns Area of Outstanding Natural Beauty online at www.chilternsaonb.org.
- For places to stay or general tourist information visit www.visitbuckinghamshire.org.

## Did you know?
- The *Chitty Chitty Bang Bang* film script was written by Roald Dahl, and the book by Ian Fleming of James Bond fame.

## Enticing Extras
- You can hire the original *Chitty Chitty Bang Bang* car and make a day of it, driving through the country lanes before the walk. Contact Pierre Picton on 01789 204300 or look him up on www.chittychittybangbang.co.uk.
- Print out the lyrics to all the songs from the movie before you go for a full belt sing a long, from www.lyricsandsongs.com.

## Rainy Day Options
- Visit the nearby Stonor Estate, with its 850-year-old manor house which has a fine collection of art, ceramics and wallpapers. Open from April to October. For further information visit www.stonor.com.

Hedgehog

- Drive south to Henley and the visit the River and Rowing Museum, Mill Meadows, Henley-on-Thames. Tel 01491 415600 or online at www.rrrm.co.uk.

# 8. Swallows and Amazons

Arthur Ransome at Pin Mill, Suffolk

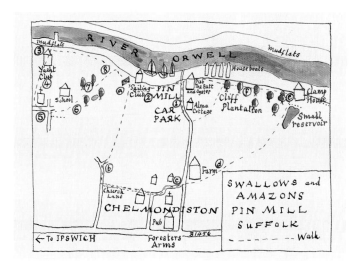

The map shows the River Orwell with mudflats, Yacht Club, School, Sailing Club, Pin Mill, Car Park, Alma Cottage, Pub 'The Butt and Oyster', Cliff Plantation, House boats, Camp House, Small reservoir, Farm, Church Lane, Chelmondiston, Pub, Foresters Arms, B1456, To Ipswich.

SWALLOWS and AMAZONS
PIN MILL
SUFFOLK
- - - - - - - Walk

**The Adventure**

Arthur Ransome's books reverberate with the stuff of truly great childhood adventure – encounters with old sea dogs and suspected pirates, mysterious places, dangerous exploits, camping, fishing, sailing and living wild and free of the watchful gaze of adults.

His books are famously set in the Lake District, but only five of Ransome's twelve stories take place there. The Norfolk Broads and Suffolk feature heavily in the other books. Just off the A12, downriver from Ipswich, is a little sailing village where Ransome set his sailing adventures *We Didn't Mean to Go to Sea* and *Secret Water*. The Ransomes moved to Suffolk in 1936, and lived at nearby Broke Farm on the banks of the River Orwell. As he wrote, looking out of the window of his study, he could see Pin Mill

## SPANISH LADIES

Farewell and adieu to you fair Spanish ladies,
Farewell and adieu to you ladies of Spain;
For we've received orders to sail for old England,
And we may never see you fair ladies again.

Chorus (sing between each verse)
We'll rant and we'll roar like true British sailors,
We'll rant and we'll roam across the salt seas,
Until we strike soundings in the Channel of Old England,
From Ushant to Scilly is thirty-five leagues.

Then we hove our ship to, with the wind at sou'west, boys,
We hove our ship to for our soundings to see;
In fifty-five fathoms with a fine sandy bottom,
We squared our main yard, and up Channel steered we.

The first land we made was a point called the Deadman,
Next Ramshead off Plymouth, Start, Portland, and Wight.
We sailed then by Beachie, by Fairlee and Dungeness,
Then bore straight away for the South Foreland Light.

Now the signal was made for the Grand Fleet to anchor,
We clewed up our topsails, stuck out tacks and sheets.
We stood by our stoppers, we brailed in our spankers,
And anchored ahead of the noblest of fleets.

Let every man here drink up a full bumper,
Let every man here drink up a full bowl,
And let us be jolly and drown melancholy,
Drink a health to each jovial and true-hearted soul.

harbour, where he moored his sailing boat, the *Nancy Blackett*, named after his formidable Amazon heroine.

In the books, John, Susan, Titty and Roger (the Swallows) stay at Alma Cottage, the pink cottage next to the Butt and Oyster pub.

The first Suffolk adventure, *We Didn't Mean to Go to Sea,* is the story of an unintended voyage across the sea. The Swallows have promised their mother they will stay safely in the harbour, but their boat, the *Goblin*, loses anchor and drifts away in a fog, sending them far out to sea and all the way to Holland. A sailing race to Holland takes place every year from the sailing club at Pin Mill as a tribute to the book. In the second book, *Secret Water*, the Swallows are marooned on an island with a small boat and left to survey and chart the area of islands and marshes. These islands are south of Pin Mill at Hamford Water.

Our walk follows a footpath up the estuary of the River Orwell and loops back to the warmth of the pub and the chinking of the boats of Pin Mill. Watch the boats sailing up and down the river and look out for the occasional container ship heading upstream to the docks at Ipswich, just as Arthur Ransome used to do. When the tide is low, the river turns to mudflats and you can walk out on 'the hard', a kind of pavement in the mud heading out where the road ends. Watch for wading birds, such as snipe, lapwing and redshank (see our bird chart on page 151). As many as fifty thousand birds from as far away as the Arctic Circle spend winter here, feeding on snails and shrimps in the mud. The recently found and restored *Nancy Blackett* still sails these waters and is worth looking out for as you walk. The woods in the Cliff Plantation are filled with sycamore, ash, elm, hazel and oak. The Butt and Oyster pub, featured in the books, is the start and finish of the walk.

**Map** Ordnance Survey Explorer Map 197

**Distance** 4.5 km / 2.8 miles for the first loop

back to Pin Mill. Add a further 4.5 km / 2.8 miles if you walk all the way round and back through the Cliff Plantation.

**Terrain** Along the river estuary and up into some woods. It can be wet underfoot.

## What will I need?
- Binoculars for spotting wading birds
- Crabbing kit for catching crabs on the hard
- A picnic or snacks. Pack Swallows and Amazons food – apples, Bath buns, parkin, rock cakes, grog (lemonade) and ginger beer.
- For the true adventurer, pack some pemmican. Real pemmican was a high-calorie survival food made from meat and fat, used by Arctic explorers. The Swallows took tins of meat instead of pemmican for their adventures.
- Rope for knot practice
- Take a copy of *We Didn't Mean to Go to Sea* and read the opening lines as you sit on the harbour side. Or sing a traditional sea shanty such as 'Spanish Ladies'.

## How to get there
Take the A12 towards Ipswich and then take the A14, coming off quickly at Junction 56. Turn left on the B1456 to Shotley and keep following signs to the B1456. Drive through Freston and into Chelmondiston. At the Foresters Arms pub, turn left to Pin Mill. Drive down the narrow, winding lane and park in the car park on the left, before the harbour.

## What can we listen to on the way?
- A CD audiobook of *Swallows and Amazons* (abridged) by Gabriel Woolf is available. He has recorded the entire series of Ransome's books on to cassette and is slowly transferring them to CD. *Great Northern* has just been completed. For more details visit www.swallows-and-amazons.com.

## SEMAPHORE

Nancy Blackett, leader of the Amazons, sent secret messages to her friends by drawing people signalling in semaphore code. Learn the flag signals and send messages to each other across from hill top to valley.

Arms are good, flags are better. Make some simple flags from sticks and handkerchiefs and practise your semaphore like the Swallows and Amazons.

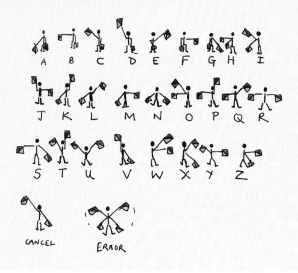

### Walk the Walk

**1** Turn left on to the lane from the car park, down to the harbour. The Butt and Oyster is on your right. It may be worth popping in to reserve a table and to check when they are taking last orders for lunch. Turn left and walk along the front, straight on past Harry King and Sons Boat Repairs, towards the Pin Mill Sailing Club. Follow the lane as it bends round the cottages.

**2** Take the first turning on the right, at the double garages, on to a marked footpath. Follow this path in a straight line along the river's edge. Drop down to explore whenever you want on small paths that cut through the hedgerow, returning to the main footpath to carry on. Keep going until you reach the Royal Harwich Yacht Club, about a mile later.

**3** At the Yacht Club, walk straight on, around the front of the Club House, and follow the path to the tarmac road. Turn left and walk up the road.

**4** Just after the Club car park, turn left on to a footpath into the woods. As the footpath opens up, take the left fork and carry straight on along the lightly wooded valley.

**5** The path crosses a playing field, curling around the church and left to a crossroads in front of the church gate. Turn right and you will see two stiles in immediate succession along the fence. Take the first stile and cut through the fields in front of the imposing Ipswich School.

**6** After the school, climb over another stile and follow the path to the left through the middle of an arable field and into the woods.

**7** Follow the wide track through the woods, passing a pond on your right. Skirt a field and keep going on the track, now looking down at the river again on your left. Keep going straight on, on a smaller path into the open field, leaving the wide track bending

## CRABBING

All you need to go crabbing is a fishing line, a weight to hang on the line, some bacon (or similar) as bait, and a bucket of water to put the crabs in. Simply unravel a long stretch of line and tie your weight to the end of it. A hag stone (a stone with a hole in it) is perfect for the job. Tie the bait to the line and then dangle the whole thing into the sea at the end of a quay, jetty or off a harbour wall. Pull the line up every now and then and see what you've got.

Sometimes you will have several crabs hanging from the line, or maybe just one big one. Haul it in and put your catch in the bucket of water. When you think you have enough crabs for a race, take the bucket up the beach and set them free. See how quickly they race back to the water. Give them names and allocate teams for added sport.

*Crab*

away to the right.

**8** This path rejoins the path you set off on. Retrace your steps back to Pin Mill, passing through a gate and eventually past the Sailing Club and into the village.

**If you wish to extend the walk**, you can follow the footpaths behind the village and back through the Cliff Plantation to the pub.

**a** After rejoining the path, at point 8, walk straight on to the gate, towards Pin Mill. But after the gate, turn right, heading up the hill. Keep going straight on until you come to a tarmac lane.

**b** Walk to the junction and turn left. After 200 m / 220 yards, turn left along a footpath that leads to the village. Pop out on the edge of the village and head straight on, towards the church.

**c** At the church, follow the lane left down the hill to a T-junction. Walk straight across, taking care of cars, and up a bridleway to Hill Farm.

**d** Walk straight on, past the farm, with the farm buildings on your

curlew

left. The track is now on flat land with big skies, full of good puddles to splash through after rain. Cold and windy in winter, baking in summer. Follow it across the fields for 1.5 km / 1 mile, and then head left down past a small reservoir to the right. Go straight on all the way to the river.

**e** When you reach Clamp House, take the footpath to the left, into the Cliff Plantation. This is part of the Stour and Orwell walk. The woods are full of interesting trees to climb and enormous gnarled gorse bushes, tempting to hide in.

**f** Keep walking on a virtually straight path back to Pin Mill through the Cliff Plantation.

If the tide is out, drop down to your right and take the lower path past some extraordinary ramshackle and rusty houseboats, perfect for old sea dogs, emerging in front of the Butt and Oyster.

If the tide is high, stay on the upper path and follow the footpath out through the bungalows and down the steps to the lane. Turn right on the lane and walk down to the harbour.

### Eat Me, Drink Me
• The Butt and Oyster Pub, Pin Mill. Tel 01473 780764. This pub, at the start and finish of the walk, is great, with good food, ale and hot chocolate. At high spring tides, you can order a pint through the window without leaving your boat. Legend links the pub to tales of smuggling and skulduggery. Open from 11 a.m. to 11.30 p.m. every day. Food served from 12 p.m. to 2.30 p.m. and from 6.30 p.m. to 9.30 p.m.

### Useful Information
• For tourist information and a list of places to stay visit www.suffolkcoast.co.uk.
• For the story of the *Nancy Blackett* visit www.nancyblackett.org.
• Visit the Arthur Ransome website at www.arthur-ransome.org.

**Did you know?**
- Arthur Ransome travelled to Russia in 1913 to study folk tales. He stayed on, working as a newspaper reporter and was a witness to the Russian Revolution. He was close to Russia's leaders, playing chess with his friend Lenin. He met his future wife, Trotsky's secretary Evgenia Shelepina, in Moscow. Together, they made a dramatic escape from war-torn Moscow.

**Enticing Extras**
- Next to the pub is the Pin Mill Studio, an art gallery and shop selling the work of local artists, pottery, paintings and photographs of Suffolk. It also offers art and craft activities for kids. You can, if you are having a terrible day or the rain pours down, set your children up with an art activity for while. Tel 01473 780130.
- Pin Mill Sailing Club is just upriver from the pub. Tel 01473 780271 or online at www.pmsc.org.uk. The sailing here is mainly for day boats and cruisers. The club offers mooring.

**Rainy Day Options**
- Escape from the rain in the Butt and Oyster and play board games, provided by the pub. Get a pack of cards and, as they do in *Peter Duck,* play Miss Milligan's Patience, otherwise known as Racing Demon.

# 9. Flopsy, Mopsy, Cottontail and Peter

Beatrix Potter at Camfield Place, Hertfordshire

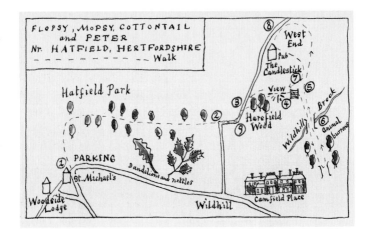

## The Adventure

This is a visit to Hertfordshire and the countryside that inspired Beatrix Potter to write some of her beloved children's books, including *Peter Rabbit*. Every summer, as a child, Potter came to stay with her grandparents at Camfield Place, a house that her grandfather built in 1867. It probably had a vegetable garden just like Mr McGregor's. We are looking round the nearby woods and fields for rabbits and their burrows. See if you can find one in the sandy soil under some tree roots just like the one Peter and his sisters lived in. We are also foraging for edible wild plants to eat just as Flopsy, Mopsy, Cottontail and Peter would have done. The sorts of things we hope to find are: dandelions to put into salad, stinging nettles to make soup, elderflowers to make cordial, and wild rose petals for jam making. As there are plenty of blackberry

bushes, if you visit in the autumn it should be possible to
have blackberries and milk for your tea just like Peter
Rabbit's siblings unless like poor old Peter you have a
tummy ache and have to be sent to bed with some
camomile tea. If you've got sharp eyes you might also see lots
of animal tracks, and some wild animals: we saw a deer, rabbits and
lots of hedgerow and game birds. Another thing to think about whilst
you are here is conservation as Beatrix Potter, as well as being a
great storyteller and illustrator, was an early campaigner for
conservation. She donated some of her earnings to the fledgling
National Trust. So think carefully about the environment as you walk
around. Don't pick anything you shouldn't and don't leave any litter.

**Map** Ordnance Survey Explorer Map 182

**Distance** 8 km / 5 miles

**Terrain** Easy, well-managed paths, a short bit on tarmac lanes plus
a rather rootbound wooded path. If you've got very little ones a
walk to the brook and back would be enough.

### What will I need?
• A picnic (although there is a pub halfway round)
• Gloves for picking stinging nettles and other foodstuffs
• A bag for collecting wild food
• A sketchbook. Even if you don't manage much drawing out in the
  field, you could collect a few specimens to make a nature
  notebook when you get home. Try and draw some of the things
  you have found or find inspiration in their patterns and colours.
• A scavenger hunt list (see pages 78 and 163 for suggestions)

### How to get there
A1(M) to Junction 2. Take the A1001 direction Hatfield. Then take
A1000 direction Potters Bar. Take the first left off the A1000

signposted Wildhill and Woodside. Once you pass Woodside Lodge, the gatehouse of a country estate, you need to slow down. Shortly afterwards and just opposite the second lane on the right you will see a gravel drive. Drive just beyond here and pull up on a grass verge just after some black gates. As you are parking near houses please be sensitive to the residents. The walk starts on the gravel footpath to the right of the house you have passed just before parking your car.

## What can we listen to on the way?
- *Beatrix Potter Favourite Tales: The Tales of Peter Rabbit and Jemima Puddle-Duck* (Frederick Warne and Co.)
- *The World of Beatrix Potter* (Penguin)

## Walk the Walk
1 Walk down the footpath that runs down the right-hand side of the house. This starts off as a well-defined gravel footpath – it looks slightly like private property but soon becomes a woodland path. At a split in the path keep left.
2 At the tarmac lane go straight and walk on 200 m / 220 yards.
3 After a bend in the road take a right signposted 'public byway' off the road into the woods. Follow this path, heading straight on.
4 Keep looking through the trees on your right over the fields until you can see Camfield Place, Beatrix Potter's grandparents' house, in the distance.
5 Just after you've been able to see the house there is a wooden kissing gate on the right. Turn right and follow the path around the field. In the autumn this is a great place to pick blackberries.
6 Cross a small bridge over Wildhill Brook and walk alongside the brook listening out for the sound of it babbling – you might have to stand completely still to hear it. Look out for the numerous animal burrows and build a fairy garden among the moss-covered riverbanks. This would be a good spot to have a picnic.

Nettle.

## FORAGING FOR FOOD

This is fun to do and anyone can do it. On this adventure we are looking for a few specific things: stinging nettles, blackberries, elderflower (pictured below), dandelions and wild rose petals. There are some recipes to try on page 200.

### Nettle Facts

- Did you know that nettles are full of vitamins A and C?
- Always pick the young leaves at the top of the plant as they will be more tender than those at the bottom.
- Think about where you are picking if you really plan to eat it, i.e. not too near crop-sprayed fields or within dog peeing reach.
- Don't eat raw nettles: cooking them neutralises the stinging agent in the plant.
- You can cook and eat nettles just like spinach.
- Green leaves taste much more bitter to children than adults. This may be evolutionary: the bitter taste acts as a deterrent to children and prevents them from eating things that might be poisonous.

When you arrive at the next bridge turn back and retrace your steps. Come out through the kissing gate back on to your original path.

**7** Turn right and follow the track as it climbs slightly uphill. Keep going straight until you come to West End Farm and a tarmac lane. Veer left and continue. See if you can spot the Victoria Regina post box.

**8** Just after the bend in the road you will come to the Candlestick pub. Stop here if you're short of supplies (see below for details); if not turn left on the footpath just before the pub. Walk down the hill following the footpath as it drops back to join the main path. At the main path turn right and retrace your steps all the way back to the lane.

**9** Turn left at the lane and walk down to the bend in the road, then take the footpath on the right signposted Green Street and Wildhill Road ¾ mile. This is the same path as before, and will take you all the way back to your car.

---

### CREATING A FAIRY WORLD

Gather small stones, moss and leaves to create a miniature world where fairies and elves might live. Make a small house with stones, using leaves for the roof. Make a tiny pond with water from a nearby stream and float petals on it.

---

### Eat Me, Drink Me

- Candlestick Pub, West End, Hatfield, Hertfordshire.
  Tel 01707 261322.

### Useful Information

- For further information on nettles and all things nettle related visit www.nettles.org.uk.
- Read *Food for Free* by Richard Mabey (Collins).
- For further information on Beatrix Potter go to www.peterrabbit.com or www.beatrixpottersociety.org.uk, or visit the Victoria and Albert Museum online at www.vam.ac.uk.
- To buy the books and audio CDs go to www.bookspeterrabbit.com.

### Did you know?

- Beatrix Potter had a pet Belgian buck rabbit called Peter Piper who was bought in the Uxbridge Road, Shepherd's Bush for 4s.6d.
- The wild rose (or dog rose) is England's national flower.

# 10. Walking with Raptors

Christmas Common, Oxfordshire

WALKING WITH RAPTORS
RED KITES at CHRISTMAS COMMON
OXFORDSHIRE
– – – – – – – – – – – – – – Walk

**The Adventure**

This is where the red kite was reintroduced to Britain after disappearing from our landscape, hunted out of existence, in the nineteenth century. Between 1989 and 1994, pairs of red kites were brought over from Spain to The Chilterns. Now the bird is thriving, with over two hundred breeding pairs. This is one of the greatest success stories of wildlife conservation. You will see dozens of pairs on this walk. The red kite is least active from July to September, and its fine tail is ragged and moulting, so make this a spring, autumn or winter expedition for the best sightings. Time it for the wild cherries and bluebells in the woods, while the trees are still bare. Or come in the autumn and look out for berries and hips in the hedgerows. The crisp, clear days of winter are the very best for kite spotting.

The red kite is a magnificent bird of prey and has very distinctive markings, with its red-brown body, sharply angled wings and a striking deep fork in its tail. Watch them glide, often in pairs, soaring over the woods and meadows, looking for carrion. They mostly scavenge, but they also prey on small mammals, insects and worms. They have a strange, high-pitched cry that now echoes through The Chilterns.

**Map** Ordnance Survey Explorer Map 171

**Distance** 5 km / 3 miles

**Terrain** Wooded walk with bluebells

**What will I need?**
- Binoculars for a closer look at these beautiful birds of prey
- A bag for collecting berries

**How to get there**

Take the M40 out of London to Junction 5. Then take the A40 towards Stokenchurch. After you cross back over the motorway, immediately turn left on the A40 towards Oxford. Take the first left, signposted to Christmas Common. The village is 5 km / 3 miles from here. The Fox and Hounds pub is on your right. Park on the verge in front of the pub or in the car park if you are ending up here. Pop in and book for lunch or phone ahead of time.

## What can we listen to on the way?
- *Geoff Sample Bird Songs and Calls* available from www.rspb.org.uk.
- *The Bad Bird Watcher's Companion* by Simon Barnes (Naxos)

## Walk the Walk
**1** With the pub on your right, walk a short way along the road. Shortly after a row of modern cottages and a beech hedge, you will see a small sign on your left saying Oxfordshire Way in the hedgerow, leading you into Queen Wood. There is an unusual church just beyond the hedge. Take this path and walk through the woods, heading across to the other side of the wood.

**2** Pop out of the woods next to a cottage called Prior's Grove. Wiggle to the left and walk out on to a quiet lane. Turn right here, past some neat cottages and houses on your right.

**3** The lane leads you to a sign for Queen and College Wood. Walk straight on, ambling through the woods on an ancient track for a while. Children can clamber along the path above the track. Look out for dogwood roses, hawthorn and juniper in the hedgerows.

**4** After leaving the wood, there is a crossroads of walking paths, just before a farm. We will come back to this point later in the walk, but for now, turn right over the stile and across the field, following the Oxfordshire Way. Head for another stile on the edge of a wood. Climb over and into the wood.

**5** The path soon splits. Take the narrower path to the right, dropping down through the

Red Kite

woods, eventually reaching a beautiful glade, perfect for a picnic and several games of 40/40 or Cocky Olly. Or just for ambushing and battles.

**6** The second path to your right out of the glade takes you to a valley where in autumn and early winter the red kites gather and swoop low in the woods. Listen out for their distinctive mewing and whistling. This is a perfect place for spotting. The low ground is also full of wildlife. Grouse and pheasant reared for shoots splutter suddenly out of the bushes and fly across your path.

There is no good way out of the woods and back to Christmas Common from here, so go back up the hill the way you came, back across the stile and over the field to the crossroads.

**7** This time, at the crossroads, go straight across into the opposite field, with the farm on your right. The path hugs the edge of the hedgeline until it cuts diagonally left across the middle of the grassy field, downhill towards Fire Wood. Look out for chunks of flint in the chalky soil.

**8** The path into the wood is marked Chiltern Way. Turn left at the crossroads at the bottom of the hill. Walk through the woods for a

## ORGANISE A NATURE SCAVENGER HUNT

Gather:
A round stone
A feather
A seed
A thorn
A bone
A piece of eggshell
A pine cone
A dandelion clock
Nuts and berries

Identify:
An animal track
A bird's footprint
An animal burrow
A bird's nest
Wild flowers
Mushrooms and toadstools
A birdsong
A wild animal
Animal droppings

while until you reach a clearing with two paths ahead.

**9** Take the smaller, grassy path to the right, sticking to the bridleway. The wood is filled with wild bluebells, so it's worth coming here in late spring. Among the woody paths are cartridge cases from pheasant shoots. Get the children to collect them as you go.

At the wooden fence, take the left path up through more woods. This will soon take you back to the lane.

Take a right on to the lane, retracing your steps past the cottages, turning left at Prior's Grove cottage into Queen Wood and then taking the right-hand path back to Christmas Common and the pub.

## Eat Me, Drink Me
• Have lunch at the Fox and Hounds on Christmas Common. They serve seasonal food and organic beers. Children can eat off the main menu for half price. Local eggs for sale. Essential to book in advance at weekends and on bank holidays. Lunch is served from 12 p.m. to 3ish on Saturday and Sunday. Tel 01491 612599.

## Useful Information
• For more about the local area visit www.visitsouthoxfordshire.co.uk.
• For more on the red kite in The Chilterns, look at www.redkites.co.uk or www.chilternsaonb.org.
• For more twitching information on the red kite and bird conservation visit www.rspb.org.uk.

## Did you know?
• Red kites steal clothes from washing lines. Teddy bears have been found in their nests, probably mistaken for small creatures. What a very disappointing feast.

## Rainy Day Options
• Visit the nearby Stonor Estate, with its 850-year-old manor house with a fine collection of art, ceramics and wallpapers. Open from April to October. For more information visit www.stonor.com.
• Drive south to Henley and the visit the wonderful River and Rowing Museum, Mill Meadows, Henley-on-Thames. Tel 01491 415600 or online at www.rrrm.co.uk.

# 11. watership down

Kingsclere, Hampshire Downs

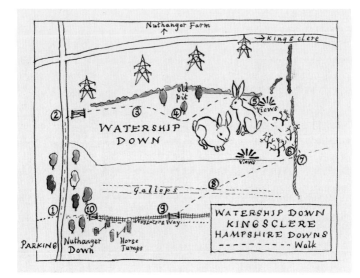

**The Adventure**

Follow in the footsteps of Fiver, Hazel and Bigwig. This is the place where the rabbits of Sandleford Warren finally found sanctuary after their Homerian adventures. Richard Adams based *Watership Down* on the stories he used to tell to his children on walks in this countryside. The real thrill with this walk is that the names in the book are also on the map. Adams was not only inspired by the landscape, but also used it literally. Anyone who can recall the terror of the rabbits' Efrafan enemies, and their escape from the barns of Nuthanger Farm to the haven of Watership Down can see it all. The beech trees, the view from the top of the Down, the wild flowers, they are all straight from the pages of the book. Scan the skies for sight or sound of the eccentric bird, Kehaar, the black-headed gull who was friend and ally to Bigwig, Hazel and Fiver. Signs of the warren are everywhere. Sit still on the slopes of the Down and you will almost certainly see rabbits, especially in the early morning and early evening.

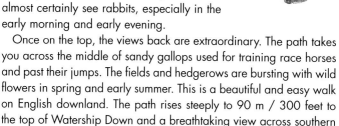

Once on the top, the views back are extraordinary. The path takes you across the middle of sandy gallops used for training race horses and past their jumps. The fields and hedgerows are bursting with wild flowers in spring and early summer. This is a beautiful and easy walk on English downland. The path rises steeply to 90 m / 300 feet to the top of Watership Down and a breathtaking view across southern England. As Fiver said, 'You can see all the world from here.'

**Map** Ordnance Survey Explorer Map 144

**Distance** 3.5 km / 2 miles

**Terrain** Uneven, sloping meadow, quite hard going in places just because there isn't a wide path of any kind. Short, steep climb to the ridge. Flat and easy across the top.

### What will I need?
- A picnic
- A copy of *Watership Down*
- Binoculars

### How to get there
Take the M3 to Junction 6 at Basingstoke. Head north on the A339 towards Newbury and follow the signs to Kingsclere. At the centre of Kingsclere, turn left just before St Mary's church, down Swan Street. Take the first right at the ducks warning sign, over a small bridge and up Bear Hill. Turn left at the junction, towards Sydmonton. Follow this

road until you reach a small crossroads. Turn left here, towards Ashley Warren and drive to the top of the hill, until you see the fingerpost marked Wayfarer's Walk footpath on your right by a gate, after about a mile. Pull on to the gravel verge and park.

## What can we listen to on the way?

- *Watership Down* by Richard Adams narrated by Andrew Sachs (Puffin)
- Art Garfunkel singing 'Bright Eyes' from the *Watership Down* movie. For the words to the song visit www.lyricsandsongs.com.

## Walk the Walk

**1** From where you've parked, walk back down the lane for 500 m/ 550 yards. The beech trees offer a quiet verge to walk along.

**2** As you go down the hill, you will see on the right a five-bar metal gate with barbed wire on the top and a small wooden latch gate next to it. This is the entrance to Watership Down and it can be quite overgrown with stinging nettles so you will have to be brave. There are no signs, no markings of any kind here, but don't be put off. Watership Down is CROW public access land and you can wander freely on it. Go through the gate, and pick your way to the bottom of the hill. It is only overgrown for about 20 or so yards.

**3** Walk along the bottom of the hill, finding occasional sheep paths to follow. Take your time and enjoy the downland. Keep the fence line and trees to your left. This place is exactly as described in the book. In the far fields, across the line of trees, you can see the electricity pylons that separated the world of man from the world of the animals. This was the route by which the rabbit Fiver and his friends escaped from Nuthanger Farm to Watership Down.

Red Admiral

**4** Halfway along Watership Down, if you haven't already been tempted to climb, you will come across a deep dip or grassy hollow (a former pit) to your left, with a few trees and hiding places in it. This is a good place for games and a picnic. If you want, you

can climb the hill just above here, and you will be directly opposite Nuthanger Farm in the field beyond: you can just make it out at the end of the track.

Look out for rabbit holes and hazelnut trees, elderflower and poppies. Those of you with small ones may wish to amble slowly back from here and cut out the rest of the walk. Otherwise, keep going along the bottom of the hill.

**5** After a good stretch over this rather bumpy, grassy terrain, you will see a path in the grass heading diagonally uphill to the top corner of Watership Down and some low thorn trees. You can tell you are in the right place as there is a hedgerow cutting across the fields opposite. The view of the fields beyond is fabulous.

**6** You will reach the top corner of the field – take care as the trees have sharp thorns. Right in this top corner, where the two fences meet, climb over where there is no barbed wire, taking care not to damage it in any way. This is perfectly fine – the Countryside and Rights of Way Act of 2000 allows CROW public land to be accessed in this way, even if there is not a stile.

**7** At exactly this point, join the public footpath, turning right, over a stile and into a large, flat field on the top of the hill, used as a racehorse gallop. Follow the fingerpost towards the gallops.

**8** At the number three sign on the gallop, follow the direction of the

## WATCH FOR WILDLIFE

If you look carefully, evidence of wildlife is all around you when you walk. Look out for feathers, chewed pine cones, nuts or seeds and broken eggshells. Look out for low tunnels in the bushes that cut across the footpath and look for tracks in the mud. If you find any, sketch or photograph them to help you identify them.

next fingerpost diagonally across the grass, towards a gate in the fencing on the far side.

**9** Turn right on to the wide path, fenced on both sides from the surrounding gallops. After a while, the path passes a set of horse jumps and bends round gently to the right.

**10** At the wooden gate, the path narrows into some woods with the trees on your right and Nuthanger Down to your left. The path is marked here as the Wayfarer's Walk. The hedgerow is beautifully stuffed with wild flowers and hogweed. Follow the path downhill and back to your parked car at the bottom. Remind children to stop before the lane as there could be cars.

### Eat Me, Drink Me

- Watership Down is the perfect place for settling down to a picnic. Bring your own or buy one at Kingsclere.
- You can pick up sandwiches and hot food in Kingsclere at the

Cuckoo Café on Swan Street. It sells good coffee, hot soups, sandwiches and simple homemade food that you can take away.

- Swan Street Stores, virtually next door, sells perfectly good sandwiches and drinks and are open every day from 7 a.m.
- The Swan Hotel, Kingsclere, is a decent pub and has a range of CAMRA beers. You can also stay overnight. Lunch is served from 12.30 p.m. to 2 p.m. only and there is no food served on Sundays. Tel 01635 298314 or visit www.swankingsclere.co.uk.
- Drive on to the nearby village of Hannington and to a country pub, the Vine Inn, for good food and a great view of the downs. Children and dogs welcome. Food served from 12 p.m. to 2.30 p.m. daily and till 3 p.m. on Sundays. Meals start again at 6 p.m. Tel 01635 298525 or online at www.thevineathannington.co.uk.

## Useful Information

- For local information visit www.hants.gov.uk.
- For tourist information and places to stay go to www.visit-hampshire.co.uk.

## Did you know?

- Halfway through writing *Watership Down*, Richard Adams turned to the book *The Private Life of the Rabbit* by the pioneering Welsh naturalist Ronald Lockley to give his rabbit heroes credible wild rabbit characteristics and behaviours. As well as his four year study of the rabbit, Lockley was famous for creating Britain's first puffin and bird observatory in 1933 on Skokholm Island, off the coast of Pembrokeshire.

## Enticing Extras

- Kingsclere has a wonderful second-hand bookshop on the High Street near the Post Office. Especially good for natural history, children's books and gardening.

## Rainy Day Options

- In nearby Burghclere, there are the Stanley Spencer murals in the 1920s Sandham Memorial Chapel. Inspired by the experience of World War I, it is an internationally recognised monument of British art. There are views of Watership Down from the orchard. The chapel is owned by the National Trust and is open from 11 a.m. to 3 p.m. Wednesday and Sunday November and December and bank holiday Mondays. Open at other times by appointment. Sandham Memorial Chapel, Harts Lane, Burghclere, nr Newbury, Hampshire.
Tel 01635 278394 or email sandham@nationaltrust.org.uk.
- If you do decide to visit the Sandham Memorial Chapel there is a straightforward pub opposite, The Carpenter's Arms, which serves lunch from 12 p.m. to 2 p.m. every day.
Tel 01635 278251.

# 12. Let's Go Fly a Kite

Hampstead Heath, London

## The Adventure

This is an action-packed visit to Hampstead Heath, an area of 791 acres of heath, ancient woodland and bog managed by the City of London. Climb Parliament Hill (otherwise known as Kite Hill), fly your kite from the second highest land point in London and spot famous buildings on the skyline. Fish in the fishing pond (licences required – see page 93) or sail a model boat in the boating pond. Enjoy some bird watching – you might even spot a kingfisher if you're lucky. Discover some of the many mini beasts that proliferate here including meadow brown butterflies. Some of the best adventures can be had from just climbing the trees and whittling sticks. There is the added attraction of Kenwood House, a neoclassical villa remodelled by Robert Adam, that has an impressive art collection by such greats as Vermeer, Rembrandt, Turner, Reynolds and Gainsborough. There is also a handsome collection of Elizabethan and Stuart portraits.

**Map** Ordnance Survey Map 173 and *London A–Z*

**Distance** 2 km / 1.2 miles

**Terrain** You can stick to the paths but it's quite nice to romp over the open countryside too. It can get very muddy.

## What will I need?

- A kite
- Bread for feeding the ducks
- A model boat or paper for a paper boat (see page 90)
- A fishing rod

## How to get there

Head for Hampstead Heath's Gospel Oak car park on Gordon House Road, London NW5. This is at the Highgate Road end of Gordon House Road and is near the railway bridge. Alternatively take the train to Gospel Oak station. For information call Transport for London on 0207 222 1234 or vist www.tfl.gov.uk.

**What can we listen to on the way?**
- *Mary Poppins Original Soundtrack* (Walt Disney) and fast-forward to the track 'Let's go fly a kite'
- *The Great Poets: Keats* (Naxos)

**Walk the Walk**
1 Walk out of the car park on the tarmac path to the right of the lido. Turn right at the crossroads, walk past a small bandstand and a café (great Italian café with excellent coffee, pasta, risotto, and if you haven't a picnic they also sell sandwiches).
2 Head left up the path just beyond the café. You will pass on your right the stone of free speech that two hundred years ago was the forum for political and religious debate.
3 Walk to the top of the hill and enjoy the stunning view. This is Parliament Hill, also known as Kite Hill, and at 95 m / 312 feet, it is the second highest natural point in London (the highest is Whitestone Pond, Hampstead at 130 m / 427 feet). Have fun flying your kite. In the autumn this is also a good vantage point to watch migrating birds such as swallows and house martins.

## MAKE A PAPER BOAT
What you will need:
An A4 piece of paper
Crayons

1. Lay the piece of paper out on a flat surface. Fold it in half vertically into a smaller rectangle.
2. Fold down each corner on the creased edge into the centre line to form the sail shape.
3. Fold one piece of the slim rectangular band up along the bottom of the triangle to form the side of the boat. Turn over and do the same on the other side.
4. Colour in your boat, give it a name and sail number.
5. From the bottom gently pull apart the sides of your boat. It is now ready to sail.

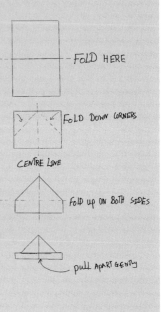

FOLD HERE

FOLD DOWN CORNERS

CENTRE LINE

FOLD UP ON BOTH SIDES

PULL APART GENTLY

**4** From the top of the hill look back down in the direction you came from and head off slightly to the left cutting across the grass. When you get to the tarmac path next to the ponds turn left. There are twenty-five ponds in total on the Heath; they were built approximately three hundred years ago to supply London with water and are fed by the Fleet River. These days each pond has a specific use: bird sanctuary where you might see herons,

cormorants, great-crested grebes and maybe a
kingfisher; model boating; men's bathing,
ladies' bathing etc. You are allowed to
fish too (you need to get a licence from the
park keeper near the tennis courts and café,

great crested grebe

and if you are over the age of twelve you need both a real licence
and a park licence – see page 93 for details). Follow the path
alongside the ponds.

**5** After the model boating pond the path does a three-way split.
Take the left-hand fork, keeping the last pond on your right. This
pond is hidden behind black railings. At the split follow the black
railings round to the right. Cut straight across the mud path into
the meadow and walk up to the far top corner. The grass is left
long here to encourage invertebrates (mini beasts) and wild
flowers. Stop and search to see what you can find.

**6** At the top by the trees turn right on to the path and you will pass
through a gateway into the Iveagh Bequest (if you have a dog
you will need to put him/her on a lead at this point). Keep going
on the gravel path straight ahead (ignoring any other paths) and
down hill. At this point look through the rhododendron bushes on
the left to see the back of a fake bridge (you will see the front in
a minute). The path then climbs the hill and you will see Kenwood
House ahead.

As you walk up the hill turn around for a view of the ornamental
lake and bridge (you may have to come off the path to get a
proper view). Just as you pass a small kiosk on your right (only
open in the summer selling ice cream) look directly over to the
other side for a good view of a Henry Moore sculpture, the *Two
Piece Reclining Figure No 5*. Listen out for the exotic and brightly
coloured parakeets that have rather bizarrely made their home in
the adjacent woodlands. There are also jackdaws here which is
unusual so close to London.

**7** Kenwood House is a good stopping-off point for loos and café at
the very least. The house is free to visit and even if you just see

one of the many famous paintings it is worthwhile. This is also a lovely place for picnic and some roly-poly down the hill.

**8** Walk past the house and look for *Monolith*, a sculpture by Barbara Hepworth, on the lawns in amongst the rhododendron and azalea bushes to the right of the gravel path. Back on the gravel path go through the gateway on your right just opposite the Henry Moore sculpture. Just ahead are some sweet chestnut trees so if it's the autumn you might be able to collect chestnuts to roast on the fire when you get home. To continue the walk you need to keep to the left-hand gravel path and walk round in a large arc all the way to Westfield Gate.

**9** You will eventually come to another gate. Walk through here and follow the path round to the left. You will emerge by a large oak tree, surrounded by a low twig hedge. Keep walking straight ahead here, into an oak and birch wood.

**10** At the end of the woods is a crossroads of paths. Walk straight across, on the path through the open grass. There are lots of lovely trees to climb along here. Soon there is another small crossroads. Keep going straight on. Shortly the path splits two ways ahead of you. Take the left path through the trees. On your left, across the grass is a clump of trees on a slightly raised mound encircled by railings. This was at one time thought to be Boudicca's burial chamber.

**11** Keep going straight on across minor junctions of paths. The path now narrows and cuts across grass, emerging to climb very gently in a straight line to the top of Parliament Hill once more. Keep walking straight across, past the kite flyers and down the other side on some wooden steps.

**12** Ahead of you on the heath below is the athletics track, the lido and car park.

**Eat Me, Drink Me**
- Parliament Hill Café (at the start and end of the walk near ponds at Parliament Hill) serves fresh pasta, risotto and soup.

- The Brew House and the Old Kitchen, Kenwood House, Hampstead Lane is a smart canteen that serves soup and a hunk of bread and sausages and mash.
- The Steward's Room, Kenwood House, Hampstead Lane sells ice cream.

## Useful Information
- For information on Kenwood House call 0208 348 1286 or visit www.englishheritage.co.uk.
- For information about London parks visit www.cityoflondon.gov.org/openspaces or www.wildweb.london.gov.uk.
- A rod licence is required for anyone over the age of twelve. You can buy this online from www.environmentagency.gov.uk/rodlicence. You will also need a free permit from the tennis hut at Parliament Hill.

## Did you know?
- Hampstead Heath was notorious for highwaymen. Dick Turpin used to ride off on horseback to the wilds of Hampstead.
- In Victorian times they used to give donkey and pony rides here.
- Many artists and poets were attracted to Hampstead, including Constable, Keats, Blake, Byron, Shelley, H.G. Wells (who reputedly sailed paper boats on the pond) and Coleridge.

## Rainy Day Options
- Keats House Museum, Keats Grove, Hampstead. Tel 0207 435 2062 or online at www.cityoflondon.gov.uk. Re-opening in October 2008, this is where Keats lived and wrote *Ode to a Nightingale* and where he fell in love with the girl next door, Fanny Brawne.

# 13. My Fair Lady

George Bernard Shaw in Ayot St Lawrence, Hertfordshire

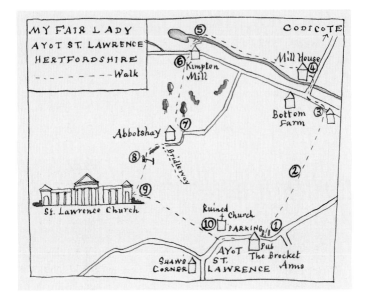

## The Adventure

Drag yourself out of the London smog and come to the country. Imagine yourself as the flower girl from Covent Garden transformed into a duchess by the irascible 'enri 'iggins. Or become the arrogant professor himself, undertaking a social experiment for intellectual amusement, and a bet. The tiny village of Ayot St Lawrence was the English home of playwright, socialist, advocate for women's rights and teetotaller, George Bernard Shaw, the creator of *Pygmalion*. This stage play was famously transformed into a musical in the 1964 film *My Fair Lady*, starring Rex Harrison as Professor Higgins and Audrey Hepburn as Eliza Doolittle.

Great for those who love a good musical, ultimately this is an adventure best suited to those who are also interested in the intellectual, political and historical. Shaw was no lightweight. On the corner, near the old church is his house, Shaw's Corner. He lived there from 1906 until his death in 1950, and it is where he played host to the great and the good of the early twentieth century. His close friend the composer Edward Elgar, famous actress Ellen Terry and writer G.K.Chesterton all visited him there. Elegant and surprisingly modest, the Arts and Crafts influenced house remains almost as he left it, with his study, his typewriter and dictionaries, his collection of famous hats, his Oscar for the 1938 screenplay of *Pygmalion* and his bicycle. Notes to the housekeeper, the scullery and kitchen are an intriguing insight into domestic life in the early twentieth century.

The garden is planted with pre-1950s traditional English garden flowers. His revolving writing hut at the bottom of the garden is where he wrote all his major works and is a gem. Shaw died, age ninety-four, after falling from a tree in his beloved garden. Picnics are permitted on the lawns.

In the village, there is also the colourful tale of two churches, one a ruin and the other a neoclassical monstrosity. The story goes that the Norman church obstructed the views of the local Lord of the Manor, Sir Lyonel Lyde, so he decided to pull it down. The Bishop of Lincoln stopped him, but the church has never been restored. To replace it, across the fields, the new St Lawrence church was built in 1778. Influenced by his travel in Rome, Athens and Smyrna, architect Nicholas Revett designed a Grecian church, far from

suited to this very traditional English village. More famously, Revett also designed the porch at Trafalgar House, which has four columns just like this one.

This is farming country with paths through open fields, along a millstream and back to a pretty Hertfordshire village and its eccentric pub, just 40 km / 25 miles from London.

**Map** Ordnance Survey Explorer Map 182

Long eared bat

**Distance** 5 km / 3 miles

**Terrain** Open fields, gentle hill, charming village

### What will I need?
- Wellington boots
- A pocketful of Shaw's plays or *My Fair Lady*

### How to get there
Take the A1(M) out of London and come off at Junction 6. Follow the signs to Welwyn on the A1000 and on the next roundabout take the B656 to Welwyn and Codicote. At a small roundabout, take the left turn to Ayot St Lawrence down Fulling Mill Lane. It's an easy one to miss, as it is a very small turning. This takes you eventually to a crossroads. Turn left, following the signs to Shaw's Corner along very narrow country lanes. Turn right down Bride Hall Road into the village. Shaw's house is on the corner. Carry straight on into the village and park on the verge just after the Brocket Arms pub.

### What can we listen to on the way?
- Original soundtrack from the 1964 movie *My Fair Lady* starring Rex Harrison and Audrey Hepburn
- Print out the lyrics to the songs from *My Fair Lady* before you go from www.lyricsondemand.com.
- Sing 'I'm getting married in the morning' in your best London accent.

### SING SONGS FROM THE MUSICAL
Get me to the church on time
I could have danced all night
Wouldn't it be lovely?

## Walk the Walk

**1** On the left, just after the Brocket Arms, there are two stone pillars and the entrance to the Manor House and Ayot House. Walk through here and turn right almost immediately, on to a public footpath that runs alongside an open field.

**2** At the end of the field, carry straight on, joining a wide track that curves round a second field.

**3** Walk gently downhill and through the farmyard below. Take a left on to a quiet lane. Then immediately right, signposted to Codicote. You will be on the road for just 180 m / 200 yards.

**4** Just after Codicote Mill House, turn left on the footpath to Kimpton Mill. The path heads up through the woods, just above the stream.
  In spring, look out for bluebells and violets. After a while the path gets closer to the stream. Keep going straight on, but look out for a little footpath that will take you right down to the stream for a closer look or a snack stop by the water. Shallow and clear, with reeds and weed, it is a very pretty spot. Look out for kingfishers. Walk back to the main footpath and continue straight on.

**5** At the kissing gate, take the path left and over the footbridge, diagonally across the field and out over another bridge on the mill stream. A good bridge for gentle Poohsticks. Flag iris and watercress are abundant in the clear water.

**6** Turn right on to the road, taking care. Then immediately turn left on to the footpath to Abbotshay, climbing gently up the hill on the edge of a beautiful, wide open field. Take the path to the brow of the hill, sometimes walking through the hedgerows. Look out for lords and ladies, wood sorrel, wild daffodils and catkins.

**7** At the top is a lane. Turn right past Abbotshay Farm. Then take the right footpath along the edge of a field, ignoring the bridleway to the left.

**8** Climb over the stile and cut diagonally across the next field, walking towards the roof of the new St Lawrence church.

**9** Climb over the stiles and take the footpath to the left, just in front of the church. The arched metal gate straight ahead takes you in to the churchyard. It is worth taking a peep at this extraordinary Grecian, slightly crumbling, eighteenth-century church.

**10** The path takes you back to the village, bringing you conveniently to the ruins of the old St Lawrence church, of a more traditional Norman variety. The gate is usually locked, but you can take a closer look by asking for the key in the Brocket Arms. Details are on the noticeboard across the road.

Turn left on the lane for lunch at the pub, or turn right if you want to explore George Bernard Shaw's house, Shaw's Corner and have a picnic in the gardens.

## POLISH UP ON YOUR COCKNEY RHYMING SLANG
## OR EVEN MAKE UP SOME OF YOUR OWN

Tea leaf – thief

Apples and pears – stairs

Dog and bone – phone

Uncle Fred – bread

Old pot and pan – husband (old man)

Pen and ink – stink

Sexton Blake – cake

Orchestra stalls – balls (testicles) *I got him right in the orchestras*

Jimmy Riddle – piddle *I'm going for a Jimmy*

Bacon and eggs – legs

Rabbit and pork – talk

Biscuits and cheese – knees *She ain't 'arf got knobbly biscuits*

Bottle and glass – arse

God forbids – kids

**Eat Me, Drink Me**

- The Brocket Arms, Ayot St Lawrence, Hertfordshire.
  Tel 01438 820250 or online at www.brocketarms.com.
  Wonderful fourteenth-century pub with a roaring fire and
  friendly landlord, Toby Wingfield Digby. Once a pilgrims' stop
  on the way to St Alban's Abbey, it is said to be haunted. There
  are plenty of tables in the gardens for eating out, too. Good
  menu with haddock and chips, lamb shanks and lentils, and
  sausages and mash on offer. They have seven bedrooms, so
  you can stay if you book in advance.

**Useful Information**

- For information on places to stay near by visit
  www.hertfordshire.com or www.enjoyhertfordshire.co.uk or
  contact Hertfordshire Tourism and Leisure on 01438 737333.

**PRACTISE SOME TONGUE TWISTERS**

Peter Piper picked a peck of pickled peppers;
A peck of pickled peppers Peter Piper picked;
If Peter Piper picked a peck of pickled peppers,
Where's the peck of pickled peppers Peter Piper picked?

**PRACTISE YOUR POSH VOICE LIKE ELIZA DOOLITTLE**
- The rain in Spain falls mainly on the plain.
- In Hertford, Hereford and Hampshire hurricanes hardly ever happen.

- Shaw's Corner. Open from March to October. The garden is open from 12 p.m. and the house from 1 p.m. There are also events throughout the year organised by the National Trust, including performances of his plays and music evenings. Tel 01438 829221 or online at www.nationaltrust.org.uk.

**Did you know?**
- George Bernard Shaw became a vegetarian at the age of twenty-five. He called himself Bernard and never used his first name.
- Elizabeth Taylor and Julie Andrews both wanted the starring role in the film *My Fair Lady*. The part was given to Audrey Hepburn, even though her songs had to be dubbed by Marni Dixon. Marni also dubbed Natalie Wood in *West Side Story*.

**Rainy Day Options**
- Shaw's Corner will sustain you through any storm.

# 14. The children of Green Knowe

Huntingdon, Cambridgeshire

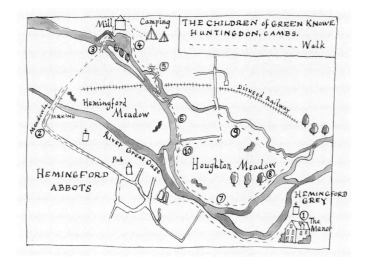

**The Adventure**

A visit to the house and garden featured in the stories of *The Children of Green Knowe* by Lucy Boston followed by a saunter along the Great Ouse. The author and her children lived in this ancient and magical moated house so evocatively depicted in the book's illustrations by Lucy's son Peter. Everything is here: the crown and orb topiary in the garden; the children's bedroom, the toy chest filled with the sword, the flute and the Russian doll; the rocking horse; the miniature, carved wooden mouse Tolly put under his pillow at night and the china dogs Wait and See. Besides this there are Lucy's exquisite patchwork quilts that she was still making in her eighties and charming naïve potato-printed textiles by artist friend Elizabeth Vellacott. Lucy Boston's story is in itself fascinating: she didn't start writing until she was sixty-two and the house is a gem. Do make sure you have read or listened to one of the stories before you go. Afterwards have a picnic on the banks of the Great Ouse, take in Houghton Water Mill, walk round Houghton Meadow and enjoy a spot of fishing.

**Map** Ordnance Survey Explorer Map 225

**Distance** 6 km / 3.5 miles from Meadow Lane, and another 1.5 km / 1 mile if you walk from the Manor House.

**Terrain** This is Fen country so it is very flat, easy walking. It could be wet underfoot as the water meadows do flood. In summer the grass is quite long and scratchy so trousers are recommended even if it's hot to avoid itchy, sore legs.

**What will I need?**
- A picnic lunch that can be supplemented by an ice cream or scones at the National Trust tea hut at Houghton Mill
- A fishing rod, or kit to make your own (a penknife, nylon fishing wire, fish hooks) and some bait. Be careful not to fall in the river as it is very deep and fast flowing.
- A tent. There is a small campsite at the mill.
- Some string and a penknife for whittling

**How to get there**
Take the M11 all the way and carry on along the A14 until Junction 26, signposted St Ives. Take the A1096, direction St Ives, and turn left at a signpost to the Hemingfords. Drive through Hemingford Grey as far as Hemingford Stores then turn right down Church Street. Park where you can, getting as close as possible to the river. Walk to the church and follow footpath signs to the left. Wiggle past the backs of some houses and as the path comes out to the river start looking for a sign,

on the left, attached to a wrought-iron garden gate saying The Manor Garden. You should be able to recognise the garden from the books.

**What can we listen to on the way?**
• *The Children of Green Knowe* on cassette only (Penguin)

**Walk the Walk**

**1** After your visit to the Manor House come back out on to the footpath and have a picnic by the river. From here you can either get back in the car and drive to the next village, Hemingford Abbots, or go by foot. What worked for us was to split up: some went by car and the rest walked. It was quite useful to have the car in Hemingford Abbots at the end of the day.

By car: turn right out of Church Lane and first left, then follow the signs to Hemingford Abbots. Drive past the Axe and Compass pub and straight on down Common Lane, which is a dead end. Turn right into Meadow Lane and park by the footbridge.

By foot: walk along the footpath away from Hemingford Grey. At the gate head across the field directly towards some modern houses. Walk in between the houses and through the village Hemingford Abbots past the pub. Walk down Common Lane and turn right into Meadow Lane to the footbridge.

**2** Cross the footbridge into Hemingford Meadow following signs to

Houghton. Pass through a gate (don't be put off by a prominent private property sign: this is a public footpath) and cut across the meadow.

**3** Go through a gate and over the wooden bridge and lock. Follow the path a short distance to Houghton Water Mill. (You can pick up a punt or rowing boat here from Houghton Boats for £6 an hour.) Houghton Mill is the only working watermill left on the Great Ouse.

**4** After the mill, turn right and walk past the National Trust ice cream hut, tea room (and loos), taking the little path on the right close to the river. The campsite is just here on your left. This is a good place to feed the ducks and a safe place for fishing.

**5** The path takes you along the meadow's edge through a kissing gate and over four bridges to the edge of the Great Ouse.

**6** You are now walking on the river's edge. Keep going straight on through several meadows and over another wooden bridge (this is where you loop back to on the return journey). Directly across the river is the spire of Hemingford Abbots church. Look out for the white willow trees along the banks and the flood meadows along the way. The willows used to be pollarded to keep them in good shape and the harvested wood would be used for thatching, basket making and fencing.

**7** The path now follows the river round to Hemingford Grey church. You can see the square tower as you walk. You are now in Houghton Meadow and there are lots of wild flowers to look for

## WHITTLE A STICK

Find a long, whippy piece of willow and spend some time whittling it, i.e. peeling off the outer layer of bark, with a small pocket knife (make sure your parents say it's OK) and then make an impromptu fishing rod. Tie some string on the end and dangle it in the water with a bit of bread on the end and see what you get!

here, especially in spring, such as green winged orchids, yellow rattle, salad burnet and pepper saxifrage. At the end of a grassy meadow you will pass Six Gates Weir. Walk past it keeping to the meadow path along the river.

**8** As the path continues, you will leave Hemingford Grey church behind you on the other side of the river. Keep going until another tributary joins the river from the left. Just before they actually join and in front of a rusty fence, turn left following the tributary up and round the meadow.

**9** Keep following the footpath alongside the tributary until you come to a large bridge on your right. Do not cross over the bridge, but veer left here, following the footpath in an arc round the meadow. Keep going along the hedgerow and cross over the small wooden bridge halfway along.

**10** You are now walking in a more or less straight line towards the spire of Hemingford Abbots church, across the other side of the Great Ouse. Just as you reach the river, turn right over the footbridge and pick up the path you came on. Retrace your steps towards the mill, over the footbridges to a well-earned ice cream.

### Eat Me, Drink Me

• The Cock, 47 High Street, Hemingford Grey. Tel 01480 463609 or visit

www.cambscuisine.com. Food served from 12 p.m. to
2.30 p.m. and 6.30 p.m. to 9 p.m. A good alternative to a
picnic if you visit in winter. Booking essential.
- The Axe and Compass, 45 High Street, Hemingford Abbots.
Tel 0870 141 3418. Serves meals weekdays from 12 p.m. to
2.30 p.m. and weekends from 12 p.m. to 3 p.m.
- National Trust tea room at Houghton Mill serves delicious ice
creams and cream teas. Closed from October to March.
Tel 01480 388588 or online at www.nationaltrust.org.uk.
- Hemingford Stores open seven days a week.

## Useful Information
- Manor House, Hemingford Grey, Huntingdon, Cambridgeshire.
Visit www.greenknowe.co.uk. The house and garden are open
all year round. A tour of the house costs £5 per adult, £1.50
per child. By appointment only, contact Diana Boston on
01480 463134.
- Houghton Mill, nr Huntingdon, Cambridgeshire.
Tel 01480 301494 or online at www.nationaltrust.org.uk.
Open April to October with working demonstrations on
Sundays. Open Saturday from 11 a.m. to 5 p.m., Sunday from
1 p.m. to 5 p.m. and from March to September on Monday to
Wednesday from 1 p.m. to 5 p.m. Last entry 4.30 p.m.
- The Meadows are owned by the Wildlife Trust. For more
information visit www.wildlifetrusts.org.
- Stay at the Willow Guest House, 45 High Street, Hemingford
Grey. Tel 01480 494748 or www.thewillowguesthouse.co.uk.
- The Caravan Club Campsite, Houghton, Huntingdon,
Cambridgeshire. Tel 01480 466716 or online at
www.campsite.co.uk. Open March to October.

## Did you know?
- Lucy Boston was mistakenly suspected of being a spy in World
War II.

# 15. Time Travelling

Greenwich, London

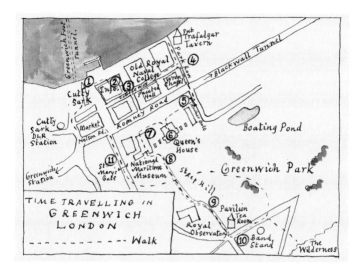

**The Adventure**

Take a boat downriver from the centre of London to Greenwich on the south side of the Thames with a glorious park and the Royal Observatory, the home of astronomy. This is 0° longitude. It is where every day officially starts. It is point 0 in time and space. This is an adventure to fire the imagination of keen historians, architects and would-be astronomers. Wren and Hawksmoor buildings dominate the landscape, each competing to be more beautiful than the other. The *Cutty Sark*, once the fastest tea clipper on the seas, is dry docked just by the river, the Old Naval College with its baroque painted hall and the Wren Chapel is next door. The National Maritime Museum, one of the best museums of naval history in the world, is at the foot of the park, wedged next to the Inigo Jones Queen's House and its fabulous art collection. On the hill above is the Royal Observatory and the newly built Planetarium, part of a £15 million Time and Space project. Come as early as you can bear if you want to visit any of the museums as it gets busy at weekends. Every museum in Greenwich is free, so you can visit them for just a few minutes, twice in a day, or plan to come back another day for the things you didn't see.

From the top of the hill, look back at the backdrop of the City of London sandwiched between the ancient domes of the Naval College and Museum. This is one of the best views in London.

**Map** *London A–Z*

**Distance** You can walk as much of the park as you've got time for. The distances are not huge, but there is a lot to pack into this trip so be selective and save some for next time. You will need all day.

**Terrain** Urban, buggy friendly, good paths

#### What will I need?
- Binoculars for the long views
- A Captain's hat and a telescope
- A watch

#### How to get there
By car from the North, take the A12 to the Blackwall Tunnel and come off just south of the Thames, following the signs to Greenwich Village. From the South, take the M25, then the A2 straight to Greenwich. There are public car parks in Greenwich Park and there is a convenient, if small, car park underneath the *Cutty Sark* itself.

Or travel by boat from central London (see page 114) and take in the glory of the Thames as you go. Leave a good hour for the boat ride. Hop out at Greenwich Pier, right next to the *Cutty Sark*.

Travel back on the somewhat space age DLR (Docklands Light

Railway) from Cutty Sark station. For information call Transport for London on 0207 222 1234 or vist www.tfl.gov.uk. Or if you want to walk through the foot tunnel under the Thames, hop out at Island Gardens on the north side of the river. The foot tunnel replaced the ferry in 1902.

## What can we listen to on the way?
- *How to be a Pirate* by Cressida Cowell, read by David Tennant (Hodder)
- *A Briefer History of Time* by Stephen Hawking, narrated by Erik Davies (Random House)

## Walk the Walk

**1** Start the walk at the *Cutty Sark*, the Concorde of tea clippers, now in dry dock by Greenwich Pier. Built in 1869, she sailed 360 miles in a day and broke all records with her journey from London to China in just 107 days. The development of the Suez Canal put an end to her exploits. Conservation work had begun on the *Cutty Sark* when a fire broke out in May 2007. Thankfully, more than half of the ship's structure had already been removed as part of the conservation project.

**2** Walk east along to the river towards the Old Royal Naval College. The Greenwich visitor centre is on your right, with a café, loos and a shop. Stop and look if you want. It is a good place to gather information on any special events happening that day. Either way, walk through the building and leave by the back door, past a replica of Henry VIII's suit of armour.

**3** Take a right on to Pepys' Walk then left on to College Way. These buildings, now part of the University of Greenwich, were originally built as the new Greenwich Hospital, for the care of wounded sailors. Sir Christopher Wren and his assistant, Nicholas Hawksmoor, offered their architectural skills free of charge to build the Royal Hospital.

Walk through the Colleges, passing the baroque Painted Hall, painted by Sir James Thornhill. It took him nineteen years to paint the whole thing. He was paid by the yard. The Painted Hall is also where Admiral Lord Nelson's body was brought to lie in state after his victorious death at the Battle of Trafalgar. The Wren Chapel is next on your right with its magnificent acoustics and organ. You can visit both buildings for no charge. The chapel has a service, open to anyone, every Sunday at 11 a.m. These buildings have been used in countless movies, from *Four Weddings and a Funeral* to *The Mummy Returns*.

**4** At the end of the College, you can take a left and walk down to look at the river at The Trafalgar Tavern, immortalised by Dickens and Thackeray, with its rather fine statue of Nelson. Or turn right towards Greenwich Park.

**5** Cross the main road to the park and walk in through Anchor Gate on that corner, so named after the giant anchor.

**6** Cut across to the magnificent Queen's House in the centre. This wonderful Inigo Jones designed building is now stuffed with an art collection to rival central London. Amongst many works, it has a Tudor gallery, paintings of Cook's adventures in the South Seas and Turner's famous *Battle of Trafalgar*. The design of the Greenwich Hospital was changed, so as not to spoil the view of the Thames from Queen's House.

**7** The next building along is the National Maritime Museum. Check

## KNOTS AND HOW TO TIE THEM

### Figure of eight

This stops the end of a rope from being pulled through a hole.

1. Pass one end of the rope over the other to make a loop at one end.
2. Pass the loose end of the rope under the main rope.
3. Bring it round over the top and slot it through the original loop.
4. Pull tight.

### A Bowline Knot

1. Take a piece of rope and hold it in a horseshoe shape.
2. Make a loop towards one end of the rope.
3. Bring the short end of the rope up through the loop.
4. Take the same rope round the back of the other rope.
5. Put the rope back down through the loop.
6. Pull tight.

*Lord Nelson*

online at www.nmm.ac.uk for the latest exhibitions. For naval history, and anything to do with boats or the sea, this is the place to be. Admission is free. But this is an expedition in itself, so pick off a small area and prepare to come back another day.

Behind the National Maritime Museum is the Regatta Café. Well equipped and set up for exploring families: soups, tea, coffee and sandwiches to take away.

**8** Halfway along the back of the museum is a statue of Captain Cook. From here, walk up the wide avenue through the park, right to the top, to the Greenwich Royal Observatory.

**9** Explore the Royal Observatory, with its camera obscura, time gallery, meridian gallery and telescopes. Stand on the meridian line, the centre of world time, with one foot in each time zone. Visit the new Time and Space Planetarium and Galleries. If you are outside the Royal Observatory at lunchtime, watch the vast red Time Ball, on its spire, rise and fall. At 12.55 p.m., it is halfway. At 12.58 p.m., it is at the top. At exactly 1 p.m., it drops. The Time Ball was built high up so it could be seen by navigators on the River Thames, so they could calibrate their chronometers (a timekeeper for navigation by the stars).

**10** From the Royal Observatory, turn right, passing the highly recommended Pavillion tea house. Turn left after this, and explore the park. Ahead and to the right is the Wilderness deer park if you are feeling like getting back to nature. Or explore the many paths heading down the hill. Take in the views as you go.

**11** Aim, in the end, for the far left, westerly corner of the park, leaving it by St Mary's Gate. Buy an ice cream or milkshake at the Cow and Coffee Bean parlour.

Walk back to the *Cutty Sark* via the market square that is sandwiched between College Approach, King William Walk, Greenwich Church Street and Nelson Road. It is a thriving market and very busy from Thursday to Sunday.

## Eat Me, Drink Me

- Greenwich is packed with places to eat, from the usual suspects on the high street, to cafés, tea rooms, ice cream stalls and even sausage stands in the park. We have identified key places as you go along.

## Useful Information

- The National Maritime Museum, Queen's House and the Royal Observatory are open from 10 a.m. to 5 p.m. every day except Christmas. Admission is free. Check opening times and events before you go. Tel 0208 312 6565 for recorded information, 0208 858 4422 for administration, or visit www.nmm.ac.uk.

- Part of the new Time and Space project at the Royal Observatory, the Peter Harrison Planetarium offers a star life planaterium show. Call 0208 312 8565 to book ahead or email bookings@nmm.ac.uk. Tickets can be bought on the day from the box office but must be bought before midday. The 3 p.m. and 4 p.m. slots are very busy at weekends, so aim to avoid those. The show is on the hour from 11 a.m. to 4 p.m. and lasts twenty-five minutes, with a ten-minute question and answer session afterwards. It is recommended for children over seven. This is one of the few things in Greenwich that is not free.

- The *Cutty Sark* Conservation Project Visitor Centre is open Sunday to Tuesday from 11 a.m. to 5 p.m. Free entry. For more information visit www.cuttysark.org.uk.
- For information on Greenwich Hospital and the Old Royal Naval College visit www.oldroyalnavalcollege.org.
- For updated travel information on boats and the DLR, contact Transport for London on 0207 222 1234 or online at www.tfl.gov.uk. They have information on all boats heading from central London to Greenwich Pier, including timetables. A number of river operators use these piers, so you can take any boat that is heading for Greenwich. Bear in mind that they don't always run all day, tending to leave central London in the morning and return from Greenwich later in the afternoon only.
- Thames Clippers offer a regular service and are more of a commuter boat than a tourist catamaran. Avoid the tourist services that dawdle slowly down the Thames complete with microphoned tourist information if you just want to get there quickly. Journey times seem to vary enormously.
  Tel 0870 781 5049 or online at www.thamesclippers.com.
- City Cruises offer a sightseeing tour to Greenwich. Call 0207 740 0400 for boat times or visit www.citycruises.com.
- For information on staying overnight contact Greenwich Tourism on 0208 854 8888 or go to www.greenwich.gov.uk/tourism.

**Did you know?**

- Nicolaus Copernicus was a sixteenth-century Polish astronomer who was the first to come up with the notion that the Sun was the centre of our solar system. The idea that the Earth revolved around the Sun, and not that the Sun revolved around the Earth, was a radical one and revolutionised all astronomical and religious thinking.

# 16. Roald Dahl country

Little Missenden, The Chilterns, Buckinghamshire

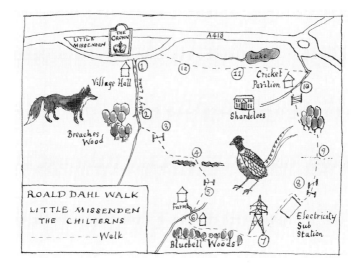

## The Adventure

Just south of Great Missenden, where Roald Dahl lived for much of his life, is the village of Little Missenden and its surrounding woods and meadows. Fill the landscape with the characters from his stories as you walk. Explore the woods, teeming with pheasant, ready to be poached by Danny and his father. Run past a farm fit for Boggis, Bunce or Bean. Spot animal holes in the banks where Fantastic Mr Fox and Badger surely still live. Have a fantastic feast on an open hillside. Pass a very grand house where the Giraffe, the Pelly and the Monkey would have been gainfully employed to clean all the windows.

Nearby Great Missenden is worth a visit at the end of the walk. On the way there from Little Missenden, you can take a quick, drive-by detour to see Roald Dahl's house. Turn left up Whitefield

badger

Lane. Gypsy House is on your right at the end of the village houses. You can only go in when the gardens are open to the public, five times a year. He wrote all his children's stories in this garden in his writing hut. He would tell his children his hut was guarded by wolves to keep them away from it.

In Great Missenden head for the Twit's Café in the Roald Dahl Museum, with its imaginative menu. An added bonus is that you will pass the old petrol pump at 64 High Street that inspired the garage in *Danny the Champion of the World* and see the timber-framed Crown House (across the road from the Museum) that was the inspiration for Sophie's house in *The BFG*. Please don't be tempted to knock on the door.

**Map** Ordnance Survey Explorer Map 172

**Distance** 6.5 km / 4 miles

**Terrain** One gentle climb, but mostly flat or downhill, fields of wheat with paths through the middle, the best bluebell woods we've seen, old farms, cricket pavilions, lakes, streams and wildlife

**What will I need?**
• Picnic for a Fantastic Feast, roast chickens, a side of ham, bacon, carrots (for the rabbits), cider and apple juice
• Take sweets for encouragement, calling them Gumtwizzlers, Fizzwinkles, Frothblowers and Tummyticklers, like the ones in Billy's sweet shop or Wonka's factory.

**How to get there**
Take the A40, then M40 out of London towards Oxford. Turn off at Junction 2 on the A355 to Amersham. At Amersham, take the A413 left, towards Great Missenden. Turn left, off the A413, at the

sign to Little Missenden, before Great Missenden. Pull up and park at the small pub, The Crown Inn, at the start of the village.

## What can we listen to on the way?

- Roald Dahl's *Fantastic Mr Fox*, *Danny the Champion of the World*, *The Magic Finger*, *The Minpins*, *The BFG* and *The Giraffe, the Pelly and Me* are all good inspiration for this walk. Try to get the versions read by the Roald Dahl himself for the authentic read, published by Collins. Puffin also do well-put-together dramatisations of the stories on CD.
- Teach the children the chant from *Fantastic Mr Fox*:

  Boggis and Bunce and Bean, one fat, one short, one lean. These horrible crooks, so different in looks, were none the less equally mean.

## Walk the Walk

**1** Opposite the pub is the village hall. By the side of this runs Toby's Lane, signposted Chiltern Heritage Trail. Walk up here, past the black and white cottage. Take the footpath ahead of you into the woods.

**2** This a deeply cut, ancient path that climbs gently. Look out for fox and badger holes in the banks. Keep going, taking the left fork where the path splits.

**3** The path opens up with a field on your right and shortly you will see a stile in the hedgerow, on your left. Climb over, turn right, and walk along the edge of the field for 50 m / 55 yards, then turn left, following the hedgerow that divides the two fields.

**4** Halfway along, cut through the gap in the hedge to the other field and follow the path diagonally across the field and along the far hedgerow. Look out for pheasants and other game.

**5** Walking towards Bunce's farm, or maybe the Greggs' farm from *The Magic Finger*, you will see a stile to your left, just before an avenue of trees. Climb over the stile and walk diagonally across the field, heading for the gap between two houses.

**6** Walk right out on to the lane. Turn right, passing Griffin Cottage and then, very shortly, turn left on to a footpath into the wood. You will now be walking through a wooded glade, filled with bluebells in early summer. These are some of the best we've seen on all our walks in southern England.

**7** Keep going straight on the path, passing a large pylon. Here the path narrows and dips away. Keep going straight on down the hill, passing an electricity substation and down to a double stile.

**8** Take the left-hand stile and cut across the field gently down hill. This is a perfect place to enjoy a picnic and a Fantastic Feast, raise a toast to Roald Dahl and Fantastic Mr Fox.

**9** The path joins a dirt track. Walk straight over, following the footpath sign. Don't follow the track left. At the clump of trees, turn left.

**10** Go through the kissing gate and turn right down the lane. This will take you past a beautiful old cricket pavilion and Amersham Cricket Club. At the end of the metal fence, turn left,

Red Fox

## BUILD A SHELTER

- Look around the woods and find three long, strong sticks or branches. One should be forked to act as a crook. The other two should be long enough to mark out the frame of your shelter.
- Lie on the ground to measure the size you need the shelter to be.
- Dig a small hole and plant your forked stick upright in it.
- Lean the other two sticks into the fork. The gap between them will be your entrance.
- Work your way around the shelter, filling the sides with straight sticks, Eeyore style, leaning against the two main branches. As they become more densely filled, find twigs with little branches off them to lay on top. These will serve to trap the top layer of leaves.
- When you think the shelter is ready, coat from top to bottom with dry leaves, several inches deep. Try not to gather soil with the leaves as this will just fall through the gaps on to a sheltering child.
- Climb inside your shelter. This should be warm and dry and protect you from light rain.

heading on the South Bucks Way through the Cricket Club and over the stile into the woods again.

**11** On your right is a small lake with ducks. On the hill above on the left is a vast mansion, Shardeloes House. It has plenty of windows for the Giraffe, the Pelly and the Monkey to clean.

**12** Keep going straight on, back along the valley floor. The path joins a dirt track to a farm and soon arrives back at the village and the pub. Turn left on the road.

**Eat Me, Drink Me**

- The Crown Inn, Little Missenden. Tiny English pub with a lovely garden in a perfect village setting. This is a good place to start or finish the walk with a cold drink, but lunch stops at 2 p.m. and there is no food on Sundays. Tel 01494 862571.
- Roald Dahl Museum Café, High Street, Great Missenden. Tel 01494 892192. Good tea shop with imaginative sandwiches (suitably titled Dahlesque creations), good coffee and hot soup. Open 9.30 a.m. to 5 p.m. every day except Mondays.

**Useful Information**

- The Official Roald Dahl website is at www.roalddahl.com.
- For details of Gypsy House Garden opening days visit www.roalddahlfoundation.org.
- For the dedicated Dahl enthusiast, there is also the Roald Dahl Children's Gallery in the Buckinghamshire County Museum, Church Street, Aylesbury. Tel 01296 331441 or online at www.bucksccgov.uk/museum/dahl.

**Did you know?**

- Roald Dahl was a daring World War II fighter pilot, flying missions in the western deserts of Egypt, Libya and Greece. He could loop the loop and fly upside down.

**Enticing Extras**

- It is worth stopping briefly at the Church of St John the Baptist in Little Missenden. It has a very unusual thirteenth-century wall painting of St Christopher carrying the Christ child.
- The Roald Dahl Museum and Story Centre, 81–83 High Street, Great Missenden, Buckinghamshire. Tel 01494 892192 or online at www.roalddahlmuseum.org. A small, colourful museum with imaginative displays and ideas. It often has events for children and free story telling sessions on weekends and holidays. Open Tuesday to Sunday, from 10 a.m. to 5 p.m. and on bank holidays. Family ticket costs £16.
- Parking is difficult in Great Missenden, so head for the pay and display, right at the traffic lights after the library, and only five minutes walk from the museum.

# 17. St George and the Dragon

Uffington, Berkshire Downs, Oxfordshire

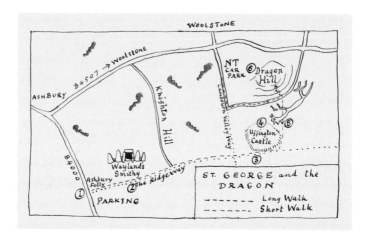

**The Adventure**

A walk steeped in history with sites to see and tales to tell whilst ambling along a section of The Ridgeway national trail that runs through ancient landscapes on a route used since prehistoric times by travellers, herdsmen and soldiers. Altogether, the Ridgeway comprises 139 km / 87 miles ranging from rolling, open downland to the west of the River Thames, through secluded valleys and woods in The Chilterns to the east. This walk is on the Berkshire Downs in Oxfordshire at White Horse Hill where there are a number of ancient sites to explore steeped in myth and legend. The first is Wayland's Smithy, one of the most impressive and atmospheric neolithic burial chambers in Britain. The second, Uffington Castle, is an impressive Iron Age hill fort commanding extensive views over the surrounding area. And on the steep escarpment just below is the White Horse itself, a 115 m / 374 foot stylised representation of a horse made out of chalk bedrock thought to date back to 1000BC. From here you get an excellent view of Dragon Hill. Legend has it that it was here that St George slew the dragon, its blood spilling on the hilltop and leaving for ever a bare white patch where no grass can grow. A great walk for story telling, folklore and battles – real and imagined.

**Map** Ordnance Survey Explorer Map 170

**Distance** 8 km / 5 miles

**Terrain** The Ridgeway is a good walking track but Uffington and the White Horse are on a steep-sided hill. It's a short but steep climb down to Dragon Hill and back but worth the effort. There is a long and short version of this walk. Bear in mind there is no shelter along the way.

**What will I need?**
- Swords to re-enact the battle of St George and the Dragon
- A storyteller
- A hat
- An extra layer of clothing as it gets windy and the temperature drops as you get to the top of the hill – unless it's scorching
- Plenty to drink
- Food and drink as there are no shops or cafés on the walk itself. The pub is a short drive away from both car parks.

**How to get there**
Take the M4 to Junction 14, turn off and follow the A338, direction Wantage. Then take the first left on to the B4000 towards Lambourn. Drive through Lambourn and Upper Lambourn still on the B4000, this time heading towards Ashbury. When you pass Ashdown House (a National Trust

Dragon

Hawthorn, May

property) on your left, start slowing down as just beyond here, but before you reach Ashbury village, there is a signpost for The Ridgeway (this cuts across the ridge of the hill so if you start going down hill you've gone too far). Look out for a car park on your right marked Ashbury Folly on the Ordnance Survey map.

## What can we listen to on the way?
- *The Dragon's Eye* by Dugald A. Steer (Orion)
- *Beowulf* by Rosemary Sutcliffe (Naxos)
- *Magic Lands: Ghosts and Goblins* by Kevin Crossley-Holland (Orion)
- *Fantastic Stories* by Terry Jones (Orion)
- *The Wee Free Men* and *A Hat Full of Sky* by Terry Prachett (Random House)
- *Stig of the Dump* by Clive King (Penguin)

## Walk the Walk
1 Head for the footpath out of the car park signposted White Horse Hill. This is The Ridgeway and takes you in a straight line to the turn off for the White Horse and Uffington Castle.
2 The first turning to look for is on the left, to Wayland's Smithy. Climb the stile, walk into the trees a little way and come to the amazing chambered tomb built in the neolithic period 5,500 years ago when people first started farming the land. It is built with Sarsen stones, great blocks of hard sandstone found scattered on chalk hills. Retrace your steps back to The Ridgeway, turn left and carry on.
3 Gradually climb the hill and whilst doing so take an interest in the geology. The ground is chalky underfoot. Towards the top of the hill, follow the footpath to the left. You will see a sign on the left for White Horse Hill. Turn left here.
4 Walk straight ahead up the hill towards the grassy mounds of

Uffington Castle. This simple rampart and ditch hill fort was built in the Iron Age around 30BC on the highest point in Oxfordshire at 260 m / 857 feet. The ditches are still clearly visible so it is easy to imagine how it might once have been. This is a good point for a picnic particularly if you need to shelter from the wind.

**5** Carry on towards the brow of the hill. Step down over the edge and you will see the markings of the White Horse. The lines don't seem to make much sense at such close quarters but it is interesting to see it close up. The horse outline was dug using the shoulder blades of cows as shovels and then backfilled with specially quarried chalk blocks. It is not known how old it is but there are many theories: 2,000-year-old coins have been found on the site and 1,200 years ago King Alfred enjoyed a great victory against the Danes there. Scientists have sampled the soils and chalk and say it is aged at 3,000 years. Why is it here in the first place? Was it a tribal symbol to warn off other tribes, a

## PRETEND TO BE A NEOLITHIC WARRIOR
- Mark your face with chalk stripes or a piece of charcoal.
- Dance wildly around the hill making loud and scary noises.
- Make a miniature Stonehenge or chalk circle.

way to show the shortest way up the hill, or a religious symbol to celebrate horses which were so important to the community? Maybe you've got some ideas of your own.

**6** Look down to see Dragon Hill where you're heading next. Take it slowly down the steep escarpment as it's easy to fall. Cross the small road at the bottom and clamber up the hill. Have a pretend battle to slay the dragon just like St George. Retrace your steps back to the car.

If you have small children and want to do a **shorter version** of the walk (1 km / 0.6 miles each way), drive round and park in the closer National Trust car park, signposted off the B4507 and cut across to the White Horse and Dragon Hill from there.

**Eat Me, Drink Me**
• The Rose and Crown, High Street, Ashbury, Swindon.

**FLINT FACTS**

Chunks of flint, a grey, glassy mineral, are made of silica, and splinter easily. They were used by our ancestors to make sharp tools. Look for ancient arrowheads or gather flints and make your own.

Tel 01793 710222 or go to www.roseandcrownashbury.co.uk. Accommodation also available.

**Useful Information**
- For information on Wayland's Smithy and Uffington Castle contact English Heritage on 0870 333 1181 or online at www.english-heritage.org.uk.
- For information on the White Horse and Dragon Hill contact the National Trust on 0870 458 4000 or online at www.nationaltrust.org.uk.
- For The Ridgeway go to www.thenationaltrails.co.uk.
- There is a great campsite which can be seen from the top of the hill at Britchcombe Farm, Uffington, Faringdon, Oxfordshire. Tel 01367 820667. They allow campfires in fire pits and facilities include toilets and electricity. £4 per adult.

**Did you know?**
- In the Middle Ages the dragon represented the devil.
- Chalk is made from the fossil skeletons of millions of tiny sea creatures. The chalk on The Ridgeway dates back to the late Cretaceous, 100 million years ago, when England was under the sea.

# 18. Alice in Wonderland

Port Meadow, Oxford

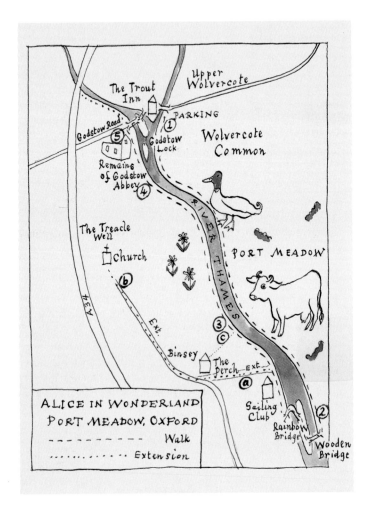

ALICE IN WONDERLAND
PORT MEADOW, OXFORD
- - - - - - - - Walk
· · · · · · · · · · · Extension

## The Adventure

We are visiting the very place on the river that was part of the inspiration behind the stories of *Alice in Wonderland*. Charles Dodgson (Lewis Carroll) was a mathematics tutor at Christ Church, Oxford, from 1855 to 1898. He befriended the daughters of the Dean, Henry Liddell, and made up stories to entertain them. These grew into the now famous book. The story is of a little girl who falls asleep by the riverbank and disappears into a fantastical world. She falls down a rabbit hole to a place peppered with extraordinary animals: the White Rabbit, the Dodo, the Mock Turtle, the Dormouse, the Cheshire Cat, the Mad Hatter, the March Hare and the Queen of Hearts. Brimming with strange creatures, nonsense games without rules, rhymes and songs, logic and illogic, death, madness, drugs and dreams.

We will meander along the River Thames at Godstow, where Dodgson and Alice rowed along, making up silly rhymes, running Caucus races, looking for rabbit holes, collecting feathers, feeding the ducks and geese, spotting herons and the occasional kingfisher and watching boats floating serenely up and down the river.

**Map** Ordnance Survey Explorer Map 180

**Distance** 5.5 km / 3.4 miles around the river, with the option of another 2 km / 1.2 miles to Binsey and back, the treacle well and a fruit picking farm. You can always do this extra leg by car.

**Terrain** Flat and easy walking along the banks of the River Thames. Can be muddy after rain and Port Meadow is susceptible to flooding.

## What will I need?

- Bread for the birds
- A fishing rod
- A pack of cards
- A copy of *Through the Looking-Glass* for

reading out nonsense poems
- Create your own Mad Hatter's tea party: pack a tablecloth, a picnic with jam tarts and a cake for an unbirthday celebration.

## How to get there

Take the M40 to Junction 8 and merge on to the A40. Keep going and at the Headington roundabout take the third exit on to northway A40 (signposted Ring Road, the Midlands). At Cutteslowe roundabout take the second exit on to the A40, signposted Cheltenham. At the Wolvercote roundabout take the second exit on to Godstow Road, signposted Wolvercote. Drive through the village until you get to a sharp bend with a sweet thatched cottage. Just beyond here on the left is a public car park (there are loos here). If you drive over a bridge and past the Trout you have gone too far. You are now at Port Meadow.

## What can we listen to on the way?

- *Alice in Wonderland,* complete and unabridged, narrated by David Horovitch and Sean Barrett (Naxos)
- Walt Disney soundtrack to the movie *Alice in Wonderland*
- *Alice's Adventures in Wonderland* (BBC)
- Those of us who hail from the 1970s can sing along to Jefferson Airplane's 'White Rabbit' for your few minutes of adult amusement first.

## Walk the Walk

1 Walk down towards the river and pass through a wooden gate. This is Godstow, the spot where the real Alice and the author Charles Dodgson rowed up the river to and from Oxford in July 1862. Walk along here with the dreaming spires of Oxford on the horizon whilst reciting all the nonsense and silly verses from the Alice stories: 'How doth the Little Crocodile'; 'You are Old, Father William'; 'The Queen of

Swan

# JABBERWOCKY
From *Through the Looking-Glass and What Alice Found There*
by Lewis Carroll

'Twas brillig, and the slithy toves
Did gyre and gimble in the wabe:
All mimsy were the borogoves,
And the mome raths outgrabe.
'Beware the Jabberwock, my son!
The jaws that bite, the claws that catch!
Beware the Jubjub bird, and shun
The frumious Bandersnatch!'
He took his vorpal sword in hand:
Long time the manxome foe he sought —
So rested he by the Tumtum tree,
And stood awhile in thought.
And, as in uffish thought he stood,
The Jabberwock, with eyes of flame,
Came whiffling through the tulgey wood,
And burbled as it came!
One, two! One, two! And through and through
The vorpal blade went snicker-snack!
He left it dead, and with its head
He went galumphing back.
'And, has thou slain the Jabberwock?
Come to my arms, my beamish boy!
O frabjous day! Callooh! Callay!'
He chortled in his joy.
'Twas brillig, and the slithy toves
Did gyre and gimble in the wabe;
All mimsy were the borogoves,
And the mome raths outgrabe.

Read the poem and be inspired to play games making up silly words or limericks using each other's names. Let your imagination run wild.

Hearts'; 'Twinkle Twinkle Little Bat'; and make up a few of your own. Recite the 'Jabberwocky' and create portmanteau words (the squashing together of two words to make a new one) as described by the walrus. Do a bit of bird watching, see what animals are grazing on the meadow – we saw cows and horses. In spring there are baby coots, goslings and ducklings on the river. We even saw a nesting coot. Try to find some beautiful feathers discarded by the birds: they are great for making quills when you get home.

Wait to have your picnic over the other side of the river where it is animal free and therefore poo free.

2 Keep going through the meadow, along the edge of the river until you reach a gated wooden bridge. Cross here and turn right following the Thames Path. Shortly afterwards cross Rainbow

## MAKE A QUILL PEN

Gather goose and swan feathers to make into quills. We found them in abundance here in the early summer months. Cut the end off the feathers and shape with a pocket knife into a nib. When you get home dip it in some ink and give your signature a flourish.

Bridge (so called because of its shape). You will pass Bossom's Boatyard, the Medley Sailing Club and the lock and lock keeper's house. Keep going straight, following the river. At this point you could pick up a rowing boat (see below for details) and have an afternoon on the river.

3 A little further on from here is the best place to have your picnic. Take the opportunity to have an unbirthday party (there are 364 unbirthdays every year) and sing the un-birthday song. After lunch entertain yourselves with a Caucus race (the way to dry off after the flood of tears). How to play: mark out a racecourse; run around madly ignoring the course; elect someone to shout 'the race is won'. Who wins? 'At last the Dodo said, "EVERYBODY has won, and all must have prizes."' Depending on the season this is also a good place for making daisy chains, picking

elderflowers or blackberries.

**4** For a shorter walk, keep going on the Thames Path along this gorgeous stretch of river with fields to the left and the river to your right and look out for rabbit holes. Quite near the end of this stretch you will pass the beautiful but haunting ruins of Godstow Abbey, a twelfth-century nunnery. The nuns who inhabited it in the fourteenth century secured a reputation for licentiousness and scholars were banned from visiting.

**5** At the end of the river path, by the bridge, you come out on to a narrow lane (watch out for cars). Turn right and make your way to the Trout Inn or carry on for a short distance back to the car park.

**a For a longer walk**, continue on to just after the Sailing Club, take the track on the left towards Binsey where Alice's governess, Miss Prickett (the Red Queen) lived.

**b** Walk half a mile up the lane to St Margaret's Church: a lovely country church with a simple, whitewashed interior, flagstone floor and echoing silence. Behind the church, among the gravestones, many being of the Prickett family, is the treacle well. Described by the Dormouse at the Mad Hatter's tea party as where the three sisters lived, treacle was once thought to be the antidote to poison and this well had a reputation as a healing well. Head back to the riverbank, via Binsey.

**c** If you can, cut back on the footpath from the Perch (after a fire in 2007 the pub and footpath were temporarily closed); otherwise retrace your steps. Turn left when you get to the Thames Path. Or you can pick up a boat here – have it delivered with a picnic and row back to the bridge at Lower Wolvercote. See below for details.

**Eat Me, Drink Me**
- Two of the best Oxford pubs, the Perch and the Trout Inn, are on this walk. Both are open all day and are hugely popular. Any weekend walkers will definitely need to book beforehand if hoping for a meal. We suggest a picnic on the meadow, and maybe a cold drink or a hot chocolate later at the pub.
- The Perch at Binsey. Tel 01865 728891 or online at www.the-perch.co.uk. Before you go, check it is open as it was burnt down in 2007 and may still be undergoing renovation.
- The Trout Inn at Lower Wolvercote. Tel 01865 302071 or online at www.oxfordrestaurantguide.co.uk/front_inn. A very smart restaurant. There is no bar food and it gets very busy. Booking is essential. It has a nice terrace overlooking the river. Also known as being the drinking hole of Inspector Morse.
- Wytham Village Store and Tea Room. Tel 01865 243800 or online at www.wytham-village.org.uk/wytham-village-store.htm. Open every day except Wednesday from May to October. The shop has half-day closing on Wednesday and Saturday and is closed all day Sunday.

- If you visit Christ Church in Oxford, there is a great tea shop across the road opposite the entrance to Christ Church Meadow. Café Loco, 85–87 St Aldates, Oxford. Tel 01865 200959 or online at www.goingloco.com. Sells sandwiches, snacks, afternoon teas and ice creams and will put together a picnic for you to take away if given notice. Open all day.

**Useful Information**
- Fruit picking at Medley Manor Farm, Binsey Lane, Oxford. Tel 01865 241251 or online at www.dailyinfo.co.uk/food/pickhtm.
- For general information on Oxford including places to stay visit www.oxford.gov.uk/tourism.
- For facts and information on Alice visit www.alice-in-wonderland.fsnet.co.uk.
- For information on Alice's connections with Christ Church visit www.visitchristchurch.net.
- The Lewis Carroll Society is at www.lewiscarrollsociety.org.uk.
- For boat hire visit www.salterssteamers.co.uk. They will bring a

boat to Godstow complete with picnic if pre-booked. Alternatively, you can call 0845 226 6396 or visit www.oxfordrivercruises.com. They will bring a boat (anything from a small rowing boat to a cruise boat) up to Bossom's Boatyard with a picnic, and you can row back up the river to Godstow. This has to be booked in advance.

**Did you know?**
- Characters in the stories are based on people Alice knew. The White Rabbit was her father, always checking his watch and running late. He left dinner every night down a private, steep, spiral staircase at the back of the Great Hall to the Senior Common Room, and this was the inspiration for the rabbit hole.
- The film *The Golden Compass* was filmed at Christ Church.

**Rainy Day Options**
- Take a tour round Christ Church, Oxford, where Dodgson was a maths tutor. £9 each or £40 for a family, under fives free. The long-necked firedogs in the Great Hall are said to be the inspiration for Alice's long neck after she drinks from the bottle. A specially booked private tour will reveal even more secrets, including the hidden door. Contact the head custodian on 01865 286573 or email custodian@chch.ox.ac.uk in advance.
- Visit the Museum of Oxford, St Aldates, Oxford. Tel 01865 252761 or online at www.oxford.gov.uk/museum. See their permanent collection of Alice memorabilia.
- Visit the Sheepshop, 83 St Aldates, Oxford. Tel 01865 723793 or online at www.sheepshop.com. Packed to the rafters with everything Alice. They say the real Alice used to buy barley sugar sweets from here. Open every day from 11 a.m. to 5 p.m. (6 p.m. in the summer).

# 19. Survival of the Fittest

Charles Darwin in Downe, Kent

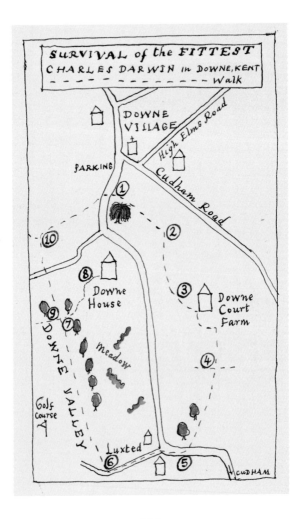

## The Adventure

This is perfect for any scientists or natural history lovers, combining a ramble in the Kent countryside through the fields where Darwin created some of the first experiments on natural selection, with a visit, via the back door, to

Honeybee

Darwin's house and collections. As a young man, Darwin was an avid collector of plants, insects and geological specimens. He was so fascinated by nature that his University Professor recommended him for the voyage to Patagonia on the HMS *Beagle* in the 1830s. This journey was the inspiration behind the theories of human origin that he wrote down many years later, while living at Down House.

The house is stuffed with birds, shells, bones and insects. It is a natural history wonderland. Darwin's love of nature was infectious and he involved his children with his research whenever he could. They collected moths and flowers from the nearby countryside and helped him with his study of bees, watching the bumblebees in the meadows as they flew from clover to clover and back to their hives. The Darwin family would often head into the countryside on walks and picnics.

This walk takes you across fields and through the woods where they picnicked. The woods above the West Kent golf course are filled with the wild orchids he studied. The best time to see the orchids in flower is May to July. The path leads right to the back door of his home and workplace, Down House. Inspire little ones with Darwin's worm experiments and greenhouses of carnivorous plants. Older ones will be fascinated to see the place where he developed the theories of natural selection that rocked the scientific and spiritual world. Clutching your copy of the *Origin of Species*, contemplate the story of life.

**Map** Ordnance Survey Explorer Map 147

**Distance** 4 km / 2.5 miles

**Terrain** Gentle, lots of stiles and open fields. Woodland and wild flower meadows

## What will I need?
- A copy of the *Origin of Species*
- Binoculars
- A bag or bucket for gathering your own natural history collection
- Go on a scavenger hunt for feathers, leaves, dead bugs and mini beasts, but please don't pick any flowers.

## How to get there
South Londoners may wish to brave the labyrinthine streets of Bromley. Others take the M25 to Junction 4. Come off on the A21 towards Farnborough. Follow the signs to Bromley and Biggin Hill, and come off the roundabout on the B2158, signed to Downe. Take the immediate left on to Shire Lane, then third left on to High Elms Road. Darwin's house is signposted from here. Follow signs to Downe. In Downe, take the Luxted Road towards Down House, and park on the roadside after the Baptist church, by a large willow tree, before the end of the village. This is not where Darwin's house is. We are walking to it.

## What can we listen to on the way?
- *Origin of Species* narrated by modern day evolutionary scientist Richard Dawkins (CSA Word Recordings)
- *Science and Scientists* by David Angus (Naxos)
- *Famous People in History 2* by Nicolas Soames (Naxos)
- *A Darwin Selection* Charles Darwin (Orion)

## Walk the Walk
**1** After the Baptist church, by the small green with the enormous willow tree, look for a public footpath sign to Cudham. Follow this in between the cottages and then along the left-hand edge of a grassy field.

### MAKE A COLLECTION

Make a collection of natural things to take home and stick on to sheets of paper with identification labels just like a proper naturalist. Gather different kinds of broken bird's eggs shell, feathers, bark, leaves, dead mini beasts, fir cones, seeds, bones or skeletons.

Alternatively record it all as you go by taking digital photographs for loading on to your computer to analyse and create a twenty-first-century catalogue of your finds.

**2** Through the hedgerow, take a footpath to the right, leaving the Shetland ponies of the children's farm behind you. Walk through a kissing gate and cut diagonally across the next open field. Darwin's house is now looming on your right, tantalisingly close. Don't be tempted to visit it yet. It is much nicer to approach it through its immaculate gardens at the back, later on in the walk.

**3** Climb over the stile in the far corner of the field at Downe Court Farm and follow the footpath signs as they navigate you around the farm. Climb straight over another stile on the right and walk out towards the fields. You will see a metal kissing gate, slightly stranded on the edge of a field. Walk through it and take a left around the edge of the field. Keep on this footpath. Look out for sloes and berries in the hedgerows in the autumn.

**4** At a crossroads of footpaths, carry straight on and then across two vast open fields. Climb over a stile into a wood, taking the left-hand path on the edge of a field and towards the village of Luxted. The path pops out on a road, so warn children.

Dung beetle

**5** Cross with care and turn right, walking to the bend in the road and cottages on the corner. Walk past the phone box and head left, down a quiet lane signposted to the

Downe Activity Centre.

**6** Just before the lane becomes steep, take the narrow footpath to the right, signposted to Downe. Keep going straight on this path, ignoring minor paths to the right. The path is wooded and gentle and emerges high above a golf course.

**7** The path cuts back into the wood and there is a crossroads of footpath signs. This is the woodland that is now an orchid sanctuary and is where Darwin and his children would often come to walk and play. It is managed by the London Wildlife Trust and has over twenty-eight species of butterfly, rare clumps of wild thyme and clusters of wild orchids. When Darwin had finished writing *Origin of Species*, he began an investigation of the orchids that grow here in the chalky grasslands and woods above the golf course. He noted how they had evolved to attract specific pollinators and wrote his next book based on this orchid study.

This is the where we leave the path to go and see Darwin's house and garden.

**8** Turn right, up the slope and over a stile. The footpath curves round, then goes diagonally up across an open field. It was in these fields sloping down to the Downe valley below that Darwin set up the first ever scientific study of plant diversity, recording the varieties and changes in the wild flowers that grew in the chalky grassland of the open meadows. Over the next stile, Down House is just through the gate on the right. A dark green door takes you through well-tilled gardens where Darwin set up his plant experiments. Some of these have been recreated, along with his greenhouse of orchids and carnivorous plants, and his beehive observatory. The inside of the house is a natural history treasure trove of stuffed birds, shell and bone collections, insects and butterflies. Finally, walk the Sandwalk, where Darwin famously paced daily in the early morning, before lunch and in the afternoon, noting his observations of wildlife through the changing seasons.

**9** Leave the way you came, through the garden gate, back over the stile and into the woods. At the crossroads of footpath signs, take a right towards Holwood Farm. Listen out for interesting old planes overhead landing at the small airstrip at Biggin Hill just over the trees.

**10** Cross the lane (cars do come down here) and rejoin the footpath on the other side. Shortly at the T, turn right, heading back towards the village over a couple of stiles and across the fields. The path narrows as it approaches the main road, popping out in the village, a little higher but close to where you started. Take a left back into the village.

### Eat Me, Drink Me

- There is a great English Heritage tea room at Down House. It closes an hour before the house.
- The village hall in Downe (opposite the church) offers cream teas on Sunday afternoons till 5 p.m.
- The Old Jail, Jail Lane, Biggin Hill, Westerham, Kent. Tel 01959 572979. A great pub and on the way to Biggin Hill. Carry on out of Downe, past Darwin's House, on the Luxted Road, past a row of white cottages. Turn right and the Old Jail is along this lane on the right. It is the old drinking hangout of pilots and ground crews during the Battle of Britain in 1940. Open all day, Fridays, Saturdays and Sundays. Lunch served from 12 p.m. to 2.30 p.m., all home cooked. Great children's play area.

### Useful Information

- For information on Charles Darwin visit www.darwinswildlife.co.uk or www.darwinatdowne.co.uk.

- Contact English Heritage on 0870 333 1182 or online at www.english-heritage.co.uk.
- London Wildlife Trust manage the chalk grassland and woods below Down House at the West Kent Golf Course. Visit www.wildlondon.org.uk.
- Kent Wildlife Trust manage other nearby sites studied by Darwin, such as Downe Bank. For more information visit www.kentwildlifetrust.org.uk.

## Did you know?

- Before his career as a naturalist and scientist, Charles Darwin went to the University of Edinburgh to study medicine, but soon discovered he could not stomach the sight of Victorian surgery and rapidly changed his career plans. While he was at Edinburgh, he was taught the art of taxidermy by the freed black slave John Edmonstone. He told Darwin enticing stories of the South American rainforest and may have inspired him to explore the world. All his life, Darwin detested slavery.

## Rainy Day Options

- Down House, owned by English Heritage, has plenty on offer to occupy you through any showers. Down House, Luxted Road, Downe, Kent. Tel 01689 859119 or online at www.english-heritage.org.uk.
  Closed on Monday and Tuesday.
  Open throughout the year (except from mid-December to the end of February) from 11 a.m. to 5 p.m.
  A good idea to check times beforehand.

Red Admiral

# 20. The Birds and the Bees

Elmley Marshes, Isle of Sheppey, Kent

## The Adventure

As soon as you turn off the main road on the Isle of Sheppey to Elmley Marsh you will see a number of beautiful birds flitting or swooping in the sky around you as you drive to the car park. This RSPB reserve has the best reputation for seeing raptors in southern Britain including hen harriers, merlins, peregrines and short-eared owls, so it's a pretty exciting place to go. There are also a host of wading birds such as avocets, oystercatchers, redshank, lapwings and yellow wagtails that come off the estuaries to nest on the marshes, and in the winter you will see teals and shelducks. The bird watching hides tend to be a big hit – there is something rather fun about opening up the slit-like windows and looking through your binoculars. Some are so close to the birds it's really easy to see them even with the naked eye. Rather usefully there are lots of identification charts pinned to the walls.

The ditches that crisscross the marsh are fringed with dense reed and sea club rush and support a variety of other wildlife: water voles, harvest mice, common shrews, pygmy shrews, marsh frogs and an abundance of mini beasts. Also look out for interesting butterflies: Essex emerald, clouded yellow, ground lackey, the convolvulus and the bedstraw haw-moths.

cormorant

It is quite a long walk to Spitend hide but it is a linear walk so you can turn back at any point if it gets too much. For an almost guaranteed sighting of raptors you will need to hop into your car and go to the Capel Fleet bird of prey viewpoint (the best time here is in winter at dusk) that is sited on an elevated mound a couple of miles away from Elmley and conveniently on the same road as the Ferry House Inn (see page 150 for directions). There is no walk involved here; it's just a case of driving and parking and taking a look. What you might see is up to twenty marsh harriers circling the skies and in spring you may catch them performing sky dancing displays.

**Map** Ordnance Survey Explorer Map 149

**Distance** 10 km / 6 miles to the furthest hide, but you only need go as far as suits your family. It is 2 km / 1.2 miles to the first hide.

**Terrain** Typical south-eastern coastal landscape of flat marshland crisscrossed with waterways bordered by a raised sea wall with an estuary beyond. The walk is easy and totally flat. Although at the coast, there is no beach access on this walk. There are lots of beaches on the Isle of Sheppey and we recommend Shellness, covered in shells as its name would suggest.

### What will I need?
- Food or snacks as there are no shops or cafés on the walk itself. There is a pub a short drive away (see page 150 for details).
- Plenty to drink

- Binoculars
- A sketchpad and pencils
- Magnifying glass for mini beasts
- Sun hats are essential

## How to get there

Take the M2 signposted Canterbury, Dover, Channel Tunnel to Junction 5, then take the A249 signposted Sheerness. Cross the new big bridge to the Isle of Sheppey. At the first roundabout take the second exit, following signs to Leysdown. At the second roundabout take the third exit. From here follow the signs to Elmley Marsh Nature Reserve. Drive 3 km / 2 miles through marshland (start looking out for birds here) to the RSPB car park at Kingshill Farm. There are loos here but no shop.

## What can we listen to on the way?

- *Geoff Sample Bird Songs and Calls* available from www.rspb.org.uk.
- *A Bad Birdwatcher's Companion* by Simon Barnes (Naxos)

## Walk the Walk

1 Leave the car park on the raised path, looking out for birds all the while. After 2 km / 1.2 miles you get to a small car park for the disabled and signpost for the first hides.
2 Follow the signpost left to Wellmarsh hide about 100 m / 110 yards away. This overlooks a pond where, apart from the birds, you need to look out for very noisy marsh frogs (prey of the marsh harrier) and in the early morning or evening you might even spot a water vole. Just by the door of the hide look out for harvest mice that are being encouraged to nest in the specially erected reed sheaf.
3 Walk to the Counterwall hide about 200 m / 220 yards further on. Although near by, it is worth doing this

common tern

hide too as the aspect is slightly different and you can see over the grazing land that offers a greater chance of seeing a marsh harrier. Look out for avocets that might be feeding in the shallows, sifting for small invertebrates. The grazing animals that you can see from here, as well as keeping the grass short, play an important part in attracting the birds to this site: the cowpats and sheep droppings attract insects that in turn attract the birds who feed on them.

**4** Go back to the main path and follow the signs to South Fleet hide, 500 m / 550 yards away, walking in the lee of the sea wall. Have a look here and see if you can recognise any birds without checking against the posters.

**5** Keep walking to Swale hide 800 m / 880 yards away where you get your first glimpse over the estuary, which offers a different habitat so you will see different birds. This is where you will see black and white oystercatchers with their distinctive long, awkward-looking orange beaks.

**6** If you've got the legs for it, continue to Spitend hide, 2 km / 1.2 miles away, where you get a spectacular view over the estuary. A very peaceful place for your picnic as a lot of people don't seem to make it this far.

### Eat Me, Drink Me

- Remember that there is nothing to buy at Elmley Marsh to eat.
- The Ferry House Inn, Harty, Isle of Sheppey, Kent. Tel 01795 510214 or online at www.ferryhouseinn.com. This is a super pub with views out across the estuary with lots of outside tables. Turn right out of the reserve up to the roundabout, turn right again (third exit) and drive straight along the road until you see a turning on the right signposted Harty Ferry Road. The pub is right at the end of the road.

### Useful Information

- Elmley Marshes RSPB Nature Reserve, Isle of Sheppey, Kent. Open daily (except Tuesdays) 9 a.m. to 9 p.m. or sunset when earlier. An entrance donation of £4.50 for a family is appreciated. For information on events contact the reserve on 01795 665969.
- For further information on birds and other RSPB reserves visit www.rspb.org.uk.
- For further information about the Isle of Sheppey visit www.tourism.swale.gov.uk/isleofsheppey.

### Did you know?

- The largest marsh harrier population in the UK now breeds on the Isle of Sheppey.
- The Isle of Sheppey, at the mouth of the River Thames, is 11 miles by 9 miles and it was to Sheerness that Nelson was brought after the Battle of Trafalgar. He also did much of his sailing from here and had a house with Lady Emma Hamilton.

## BIRDS TO LOOK OUT FOR

Avocet

Redshank

Oystercatcher

Black-headed gull

Great crested grebe

Marsh harrier

# 21. Painting Landscapes

Constable Country, Dedham Vale, Essex

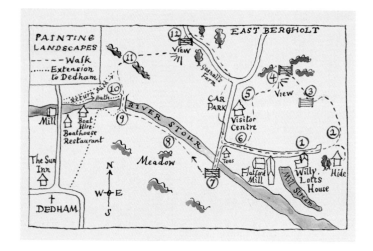

I associate my careless boyhood with all that lies on the banks of the
Stour. Those scenes made me a painter.

John Constable in a letter to his friend John Fisher in 1821

**The Adventure**

The Suffolk landscape of the Dedham Valley is the country that
inspired John Constable's paintings. He grew up on the river. His
father was a corn merchant and the family business was based at
Flatford Mill, the scene of Constable's most famous painting, *The
Hay Wain*. The mill and millpond exist today virtually unchanged.
You can stand by the pond and look across it, just as Constable did
nearly two hundred years ago. The lowland landscape with its
rolling farmland, ancient woods, sunken lanes, meadows and the
River Stour meandering gently through it is perfect for a summer's

day. Constable only painted here in the summer, when the landscape is at its very best.

The stretches of the river along the path to Dedham are glorious for a picnic or just for exploring the banks of the Stour. The river is full of fish (carp) and eels. Constable painted an eel trap in one of his paintings, *The Leaping Horse*. Water plants are abundant, including yellow flag iris and rushes. The towpath is shaded by pollarded willows, once used for making poles, stakes and sheep hurdles. The water meadows are full of long grasses and buttercups, complete with grazing herds of cows. Get out your sketchbooks or watercolours and have a go at painting the landscape yourselves.

**Map** Ordnance Survey Explorer Map 196

**Distance** 4 km / 2.5 miles. If you walk on to Dedham, add another 2.5 km / 1.5 miles

**Terrain** Grassy, open water meadow along the banks of the River Stour. Mostly flat with an uphill climb towards the end of the walk.

**What will I need?**
• Feel inspired to have a go at painting. Pack an easel and paints. Or bring a sketchbook and pencils.

**How to get there**
Take the A12 to Junction 31 and follow the signs to East Bergholt and Flatford. Drive through East Bergholt on the B1070. Out of town, turn right down a country lane and head straight across the next junction, following signs to Flatford Mill. Park in Flatford car park on the bend. Drive as far down as you can to be close to the footpath.

**Walk the Walk**

1 Walk out of the bottom of the car park, through the gate and down the lane past the visitors' centre. Don't go over the bridge. Turn left for the immediate glory of arriving at Flatford Mill and the millpond where Constable painted *The Hay Wain*. Willy Lott's house, featured in the original painting, is still here. There is a copy of the painting on the wall here to help you compare the old and the new. The spot where Constable stood is halfway between the mill and Willy Lott's house. Look out towards the trees across the millpond.

Walk past Willy Lott's house and take a right after the Field Studies Centre on a grassy path alongside a lake. Ignore the footpath arrow that guides you straight on as we are walking contrary to the signs.

2 At the end of the water, the path turns left, between a set of hedgerows. For a short detour and a spot of bird watching, turn right instead for 150 m / 165 yards to Longhurst hide. Retrace your steps to rejoin the walk.

3 Follow the path between the hedgerows until you come to a five bar gate and stile. Turn right here, into the field, following the path as it curves up to the left to a bench at the top. You are rewarded with a stunning view of Flatford Mill and the Vale.

**4** Turn left at the top, before the gate, following the hedge line to the corner of the field. Look out for rabbits.

**5** Cut through, over a small wooden bridge and make your way all the way round the field to the right, in a U shape. Ignore the two right turnings on to paths at the top corners of the field. Follow the circular walk signs right round and down the hill, cutting through the hedgerow on to a footpath bursting with wild flowers, and down to the lane.

**6** On the lane, turn right. You may want to stop at the tea rooms and collect something for a picnic or have an ice cream. There is also a National Trust shop and small exhibition on Constable's life and works which is worth popping into.

**7** Turn left, over the bridge, after the tea rooms and then turn right through the gate on to the meadow, following the path to Dedham along the riverbank.

**8** The path gently meanders alongside the ribbon of the River Stour. It is beautiful, flat, inviting country with open meadow and small bushes dotted across the landscape. The church at Dedham is visible in the distance. Anywhere along the bank is perfect for a

---

### ART FROM NATURE

- Do leaf rubbing. Place a leaf under a piece of paper and rub with a wax crayon, or paint it and make prints from it.
- Make a hedgehog picture. Draw an outline, cover with glue and stick on seeds, leaves and anything else you've found to make the body. Use twigs or long grasses for the spikes and small stones for the eyes.
- Make a nature notebook. Stick in things you have found and try and draw them or just use their shapes and patterns to create something abstract.

English oak

## HOW TO SKIM A STONE

The key to skimming a stone is three ingredients: a flat stone, a low throw and a spin on the stone. Choose your stone carefully. You are looking for a round, flat stone that will fit nicely in the crook between your thumb and forefinger. Hold the stone in this crook, with your finger and thumb curling around the narrow edge.

Face the water, making sure there is no one in front of you. If you haven't done this before, make sure there is no one behind you, either, in case you throw backwards by accident.

Turn your body sideways to the water and bend your legs, pulling your arm back. Release the stone low above the surface, allowing the flat edge to skim the water. As you throw the stone pull your index finger back, imparting a spin to the stone, as this is what keeps it bouncing. Keep score of the highest number of bounces.

picnic. Note the pollarded willow trees along the banks, trailing their branches in the water.

**9** After half a mile, to your right, is a high wooden bridge called Fen Bridge, crossing over the River Stour. Here, you have a choice. Walk on to Dedham or cross the bridge and loop back to the car park.

If you'd like to continue on to Dedham, keep walking on the path through the meadow. The footpath follows the meandering river Stour for a while and then turns off through the fields towards Dedham, clearly signposted all the way. It ends up on the high street at the edge of the village. Take a right and walk down towards the church, shops, tea rooms and pubs.

When you come back, take a different path. Walk down Mill Lane (opposite the church), past the boat hire and restaurant, cross over the bridge and immediately turn right on the public footpath along the riverbank. When the path splits, stick to the river's edge for a prettier walk, though both paths eventually join. This takes you to the other side of Fen Bridge. Don't cross back, but turn left and follow the instructions below back to the car park.

If you are not walking on to Dedham take a right over the wooden Fen Bridge. Follow the path straight on, crossing a small bridge and a calm backwater of the Stour. Look out for water lilies and dragonflies.

**10** Immediately after this, you will see a kissing gate to the right. Go through it, and set off on a grassy path, diagonally up the hill through a field of buttercups and long grass. There are glorious views of the river and valley behind you.

**11** At the five-bar gate, cross the lane (beware of cars) and take the footpath down to the right, parallel to the lane, past Gosnall's Farm and down the hill all the way to the car park where you started. You are just 500 m / 550 yards from the car. There is a brief, final stretch without a footpath, so warn those who may run ahead to take care.

### Eat Me, Drink Me

- The Sun Inn, High Street, Dedham, Essex. Tel 01206 323351 or online at www.thesuninndedham.com. A good pub with a huge outside garden and barbeques in summer. Inside there are large rooms full of sofas, games and old books. It has five bedrooms if you fancy staying over, with no charge for children sharing their parents' room. If you are staying, they can also supply picnics with rug and picnic set at £7.50 per person for a light lunch or £20 for a full meal. Order at least twenty-four hours before.

- Boathouse Restaurant, Mill Lane, Dedham, Essex. Tel 01206 323153 or online at www.dedhamboathouse.com. Restaurant on the River Stour with eating outside in the summer. Lunch served from 12 p.m. to 2.30 p.m. Tuesday to Saturday, lunch and dinner. Sundays, lunch only. Book in advance.

- National Trust Tea Garden and Shop, Bridge Cottage, Flatford Mill, Suffolk. Tel 01206 298260 or online at www.nationaltrust.org.uk. Open 10.30 a.m. to 5.30 p.m. May to end September. Wednesday to Sunday only in March and April, and weekends only in winter, till 3 p.m.

- There is also a National Trust kiosk selling elderflower sorbet and stem ginger ice cream.

**Useful Information**

- A small visitor centre at Flatford Mill, below the car park, has a good leaflet selection and loos. Open from March to the end of October, 10 a.m. to 5 p.m. From November to March weekends only, 10.30 a.m. to 3.30 p.m.
- Boats can be hired in summer from the Granary Garden at Flatford Mill. Tel 01206 298111. See the sign on the bridge. Also from the boatshed near the Boathouse Restaurant in Dedham. Tel 01206 323153. Only in the summer and some bank holidays. £11 an hour or £6 for half an hour.
- Stay overnight at the Granary at Flatford Mill. Tel 01206 298111 or online at www.enjoyengland.com. Simple accommodation for £50 a room.
- For good tourist information about the countryside around Dedham visit www.dedhamvalestourvalley.org.

**Did you know?**

- In Constable's day, barges were used to carry cargo between Flatford and Dedham. The horses that pulled them along the river had to be trained to jump over high barriers across the path, built to stop cattle straying off the meadow.

**Rainy Day Options**

- Colchester Castle Museum, Castle Park, Colchester, Essex. Tel 01206 282939 or online at www.colchestermuseums.org.uk. Open every day from 10 a.m. to 5 p.m. and from 11 a.m. on Sundays. A museum of the past 2,000 years of history inside the old castle. Originally built on the site of the ruined Roman Temple of Claudius, it boasts the largest Norman keep in Europe. Colchester was the first Roman capital of Britain. In the seventeenth century, the castle was used as a prison for interrogating and torturing suspected witches.

# 22. Puck of Pook's Hill

Rudyard Kipling in the Sussex Weald

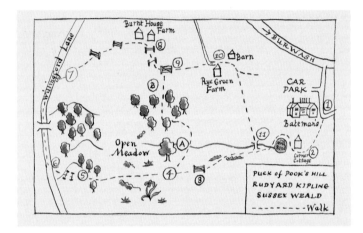

**The Adventure**

This adventure starts and ends at Bateman's, the house in the Sussex Weald where Rudyard Kipling lived with his family from 1902 until his death in 1936. Born in India, Kipling came to England later in life. He was by then already a famous writer, his books *Kim* and *The Jungle Book* and his poems *Mandalay* and *Gunga Din* behind him. The same year as his move to Bateman's, the *Just So Stories* were published. But coming to live in Sussex, his writing changed direction. The Indian stories were left behind. Kipling became obsessed with the history of England and its presence in the landscape. Knights, the Saxons, the Romans, the Norman invasion (Battle is not far away), the Domesday Book and its ancient myths and legends, all pepper his English stories. In the most famous of these, *Puck of Pook's Hill*, the pagan spirit, Puck, is accidentally summoned by two children, Dan and Una, acting out

Shakespeare's *A Midsummer Night's Dream* in a meadow near a mill pond. Puck comes from nearby Pook's Hill, one of the oldest hills in England, just above Bateman's and visible from the house. Kipling described Bateman's as a sanctuary from the world outside, and 'a good and peaceful place'. Leaving the house behind, we walk across an ancient valley filled with wild flowers, through the woods and by the streams. The path loops back on the open, higher part of the valley, with fabulous views of the Weald.

**Map** Ordnance Survey Explorer Map 124

**Distance** 5 km / 3 miles. Taking the shorter loop takes just under a mile off the length of the walk.

**Terrain** Green valley floor and gentle rise to the weald. Streams, wild flowers and mill pond

**What will I need?**
- Perfect picnic territory. Bring one or pick one up in the tea rooms at Bateman's or in the village at the Lime Tree Café.
- Come dressed up or armed with a little ancient history – Kipling's stories are filled with fairies, Picts, Roman centurions, knights, pirates and explorers.
- Take a copy of *Puck of Pook's Hill* and some of Kipling's poetry.

**How to get there**
Take the M25 to Junction 5, coming off on the A21. Follow the A21 south. At the village of Hurst Green, turn right on to the A265 until you reach Burwash. Drive through the village and take the left-hand turning to Bateman's, just as you start to leave the village. Park in the Bateman's National Trust car park, which is free if you are visiting the house.

muntjac

**What can we listen to on the way?**
- *The Jungle Book* by Rudyard Kipling (Naxos)
- *Just So Stories* by Rudyard Kipling read by Geoffrey Palmer (Naxos)
- Sing along to *The Jungle Book Soundtrack* (Disney)
- *The Poetry of Rudyard Kipling* read by Boris Karloff and Edward Woodward (HarperCollins)

**Walk the Walk**
1 The walk starts just behind Bateman's. Walk back out of the car park and turn right on to the lane past the house. On the bend is a small track to the right. Walk down here and follow the lane towards Park Farm, round the back of the Bateman's garden. Visit the house at the end of the walk.
2 After the first cottage on the right, turn right and walk through to Bateman's mill pond, following the footpath sign around it. Head straight on, walking along the clearly marked footpath on the valley floor. There is a small, meandering stream on your right.

Ignore the right-hand footpath over the metal bridge and keep going straight on.

**3** The path continues straight on through a kissing gate and then cuts through the hedgerow at a metal gate towards the end of this field. Cut through here, keeping the hedgerow on your right.

**4** Go through the five-bar gate, into an open, sometimes boggy,

## AN ESOTERIC SCAVENGER HUNT

Something sticky
Something shiny
Something sharp
Something furry
Something hairy
Something brittle
Something bendy
Something round

Something old
Something hollow
Something bitten
Something rough
Something bright
Something smooth
Something spiked
Something forked

meadow with a grand oak tree halfway through it. For the shorter version of this walk, turn right at this tree, over the little stream and pick up directions below from A.

For the longer version, keep going in a straight line, climbing the slope to the top. The path is indistinct here as the meadow is so wide, but follow your instinct to a kissing gate at the top. Look out for wild deer in the open fields behind you. This is a good spot for a picnic. The hill to your left is Kipling's Pook's Hill.

**5** Just a few yards later, cross a second stile and follow the path in a straight line across two fields, over another stile and out on to Willingford Lane, a quiet country lane. Take care of cars.

**6** Turn right and walk down the lane for about 300 m/ 330 yards, over a stone bridge and up a steep hill to a footpath sign on the right just before a white cottage and a kissing gate.

**7** Go through the kissing gate and into the field. Follow the path over a stile in the opposite corner. Then head diagonally, slightly to the left, across the next field, heading for the chimneys of the farmhouse ahead of you. You are now up on high land with fabulous views of the valley to your right.

**8** The farmer's sign directs you through a small metal gate at the very end of the field, across a paddock, to a kissing gate on your right. Burnt House Farm is on your left. Walk through to a second kissing gate and on to a five bar gate at the end of the field.

**9** Walk on, following the path in a more or less straight line through fields, dingly dells, and out on to stretches of open hillside. The path comes out on to a short stretch of tarmac lane. Keep going straight on, with Rye Green Farm cottage on your right.

**10** The track quickly becomes grassy again and passes a tumbled down barn. Climb the next stile and keep straight on across the next field. Before it ends, cut through the hedgerow on your right over a stile and a tiny stream. Head left, keeping the streamlet and hedgerow to your left until the path cuts diagonally across the field towards a bridge made with metal poles. Not a bad place for Poohsticks.

**11** Immediately after the bridge, turn left at the footpath signpost and head back to the mill pond and Bateman's. You are now on the path where you began the walk.

Walk around, back to the house. Bateman's is now owned by the National Trust. It is well worth a visit. Kipling's study has been preserved just as it was left. His writing pens, paperweight and pipe are on the desk. It is quite a dark, oak-panelled house, very English yet sprinkled with clues of Kipling's Indian past. The walls of the inner hall are decorated with bronzed, plaster reliefs of

pale clouded yellow

dog rose

Mowgli and other *Jungle Book* characters. They were made by his father, a ceramics designer who taught in the art school in Bombay. Handpainted wallpaper adorns the sitting room walls. Two sorrows in Kipling's life, the death of his daughter Josephine, aged seven, and the death of his son, missing on the Western Front in World War I, give the house a solemn air.

The gardens are as described in his books and were the setting for several of his *Rewards and Fairies* stories. His children John and Elsie were Dan and Una in the stories. Kipling used to act out plays in the meadows and gardens with his children. Bateman's sometimes puts on outdoor theatre performances to echo this.

His rather wonderful Rolls-Royce (he was an early automobile fanatic) is ostentatiously on display, just past the tea rooms. At the bottom of the wild garden is the mill where Kipling generated electricity for the house in the days before the National Grid. You can see it in action on Wednesdays and Sundays. Bateman's mill flour is for sale in the shop.

## For a shorter walk

**A** From number 4, turn right at the large oak tree in the centre of the meadow, over the bridge and immediately left, following the hedgerow and into the woods. On your right is a lovely stretch of brook, perfect for taking a moment to scramble down to, paddling or for a picnic. This is a spectacular woodland path in spring, filled with bluebells, wild garlic and the occasional rare early purple orchid.

**B** Follow the clear path through the woods until it leads you to a stile at the bottom of an open field. Climb over this and straight on up towards Burnt House Farm at the top. On your right is a metal gate. Turn right here and pick up the walk notes from number 9.

## IF

### by Rudyard Kipling

If you can keep your head when all about you
Are losing theirs and blaming it on you;
If you can trust yourself when all men doubt you,
But make allowance for their doubting too;
If you can wait and not be tired by waiting,
Or, being lied about, don't deal in lies,
Or, being hated, don't give way to hating,
And yet don't look too good, nor talk too wise;

If you can dream – and not make dreams your master;
If you can think – and not make thoughts your aim;
If you can meet with triumph and disaster
And treat those two imposters just the same;
If you can bear to hear the truth you've spoken
Twisted by knaves to make a trap for fools,
Or watch the things you gave your life to broken,
And stoop and build 'em up with wornout tools;

If you can make one heap of all your winnings
And risk it on one turn of pitch-and-toss,
And lose, and start again at your beginnings
And never breathe a word about your loss;
If you can force your heart and nerve and sinew
To serve your turn long after they are gone,
And so hold on when there is nothing in you
Except the Will which says to them: 'Hold on';

If you can talk with crowds and keep your virtue,
Or walk with kings – nor lose the common touch;
If neither foes nor loving friends can hurt you;
If all men count with you, but none too much;
If you can fill the unforgiving minute
With sixty seconds' worth of distance run –
Yours is the Earth and everything that's in it,
And – which is more – you'll be a Man my son!

**Eat Me, Drink Me**

- The Lime Tree Tea Rooms, High Street, Burwash, East Sussex. Tel 01435 882221. Tea, coffee, sandwiches, soups and cakes. Great option for high tea. Open from 10 a.m. to 5 p.m. and from 11 a.m. on Sundays. In winter from 10.30 a.m. to 4.30 p.m. Closed Monday and Tuesday (except bank holidays).
- The Bell Inn, High Street, Burwash, East Sussex. Tel 01435 882304 or online at www.bellinnburwash.co.uk. Just near the church, the Bell Inn was a favourite haunt of Kipling and is mentioned in *Puck of Pook's Hill*. Food served from 12 p.m. to 2.30 p.m. and again from 6 p.m.
- Rose and Crown, Ham Lane, Burwash, East Sussex. Tel 01435 882600. Tucked behind the high street. It serves good food, Harvey's real ale, and has a garden. It has accommodation too, if you wanted to stay overnight. Four rooms only.
- The Bear Inn, High Street, Burwash, East Sussex. Tel 01435 882540 or online at www.thebearmotel.co.uk. Near the car park in Burwash. Boasts a Kipling restaurant and has a good

fireplace. It also has rooms. Serves food from 12 p.m. to 2.30 p.m. and all day on Sundays.
- Bateman's Mulberry Tea Room. Tel 01435 883769. Inside the gardens of Bateman's so National Trust entry is required first. Open for tourist season. Morning coffee, light lunches served between 12 p.m. and 2.30 p.m., and cream teas. Eating inside and outside in the garden. They sell packed lunches and a children's lunch box to take away.

## Useful Information
- Bateman's, Burwash, nr Etchingham, East Sussex. Tel 01435 882302 or online at www.nationaltrust.org.uk/batemans. Open from 11 a.m. to 5 p.m. Sunday to Wednesday. Bank holidays and in season (March to October). Bateman's has a dog creche.
- For information on the Kipling Society visit www.kipling.org.uk.
- For places to stay contact East Sussex County Council tourist information on 01424 773721 or visit www.eastsussex.gov.uk.

## Did you know?
- Baden-Powell, founder of the Scouts, used Kipling's stories as inspiration. The pack leaders are named after the wolf cub characters in *The Jungle Book* and the Scout leader is called Akela, after father wolf.
- The private tragedy of the death of his son John, at the Battle of Loos in 1915, haunted Kipling. He wrote, 'If any question why we died, tell them because our fathers lied.' He perhaps felt guilty beacuse he had used his influence to get his son into the army, despite him being declared unfit for service.
- Kipling was a cousin of the Conservative Prime Minister, Stanley Baldwin, and helped write his speeches.

## Rainy Day Options
- Bateman's will keep you very busy until the rain stops.

# 23. Castle of Tudor Queens

Hadleigh Castle, Leigh-on-Sea, Essex

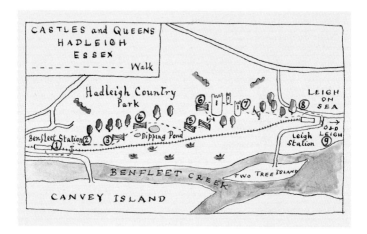

## The Adventure

Take the train to the magnificent, but ruined, Hadleigh Castle, high above the wild marshes of Canvey Island, looking out to sea. Begin the adventure at Benfleet and take the train home after fish and chips or fresh oysters at the seaside town of Leigh-on-Sea.

Follow the path from Benfleet along the grassy marsh flats beside the railway track. The trains pass regularly and provide much entertainment. The wooded valley above is full of wild flowers and you may spot rabbits, badgers, lizards, foxes or muntjac deer. A pond, specially set up for pond dipping, is just off the path, and is perfect for watching dragonflies and damselflies, frogs and toads, water snails and other pond creatures. The valley is one of the best places in Essex to see butterflies because of its south-facing, sunny slope. Birdlife, too, is a bonus here, with green woodpeckers and jays in the woods, flocks of geese, redshank, herons and avocets on the marshes and kestrels up above. Little egrets can be seen on Two Tree Island on the estuary.

little egret

Hadleigh Castle, famously painted by John Constable in 1829, was built seven hundred years ago. The ruined towers are in good shape and highly romantic, just what every child imagines a castle to be. Traditionally, it was inhabited by the King's wife. An impressive list of former tenants include Catherine of Aragon, Anne of Cleves and Catherine Parr, all wives of Henry VIII. Edward VI sold it in 1551 and, over the years, the stone was taken for other buildings, leading it to collapse into ruin. It is now owned by English Heritage and is open all year round. One of the joys is that entry is free. With the castle behind you, race down the hill to the seaside town of Leigh-on-Sea. Walk past the sheds and buy cockles, oysters and pots of prawns or head for the beach.

**Map** Ordnance Survey Explorer Map 175

**Distance** 7 km / 4.3 miles

**Terrain** Flat valley, rising briefly to castle hill. The path is quite exposed, so bring hats for sunny days and raincoats for wet ones. A longer walk, but easy going. Take it slowly and break at the pond, the castle and the seaside for a whole day's entertainment.

**What will I need?**
- A jam jar and net for pond dipping
- Bucket and spade for making sandcastles at the beach
- A kite to fly from the top of the castle hill
- A wooden sword for young knights, princess dresses for Tudor queens
- Binoculars for bird watching

## How to get there

Avoid the sprawl and traffic of Essex and take the train from London Fenchurch Street. Buy a return ticket to Leigh-on-Sea, getting off the train one stop earlier at Benfleet. Children can travel at weekends for £1. The service is frequent and efficient, but the trains can be slower on Sundays. It usually takes less than an hour. Check before you go with National Rail enquiries on 08457 48 49 50 or online at www.nationalrail.co.uk.

## What can we listen to on the way?

- *The Six Wives of Henry VIII* by Antonia Fraser (Naxos)
- *Our Island Story, Volume II, from the Magna Carta to Queen Elizabeth I* by H.E. Marshall (Naxos)

## Walk the Walk

**1** Leave Benfleet station from the main exit and turn left, heading up the main road for a short time towards Canvey Island. Just before the bridge, you will see a wooden gate on your left. This

is the start of the footpath and cuts straight across the railway line. Tell children to wait and cross together with care.

**2** Go through the white gate and up the path. At the top, turn right along the bridleway, heading east. The walk travels in a virtually straight line all the way. Blue arrows on posts mark this section.

**3** Listen out for the chimes of the bells on the boats in the estuary. Follow the path as it dips down to the right and continues parallel

## COCKLES AND MUSSELS

In Dublin's fair city, where girls are so pretty,
I first set my eyes on sweet Molly Malone,
As she wheeled her wheelbarrow,
Through streets broad and narrow,
Crying cockles and mussels, alive, alive-O!
Alive, alive-O, alive, alive-O
Crying cockles and mussels, alive, alive-O!

She was a fishmonger, but sure 'twas no wonder,
For so were her father and mother before,
And they each wheeled their barrow,
Through streets broad and narrow,
Crying cockles and mussels, alive, alive-O!
Alive, alive-O, alive, alive-O,
Crying cockles and mussels, alive, alive-O!

She died of a fever, and no one could save her,
And that was the end of sweet Molly Malone,
And her ghost wheeled her barrow,
Through streets broad and narrow,
Crying cockles and mussels, alive, alive-O!
Alive, alive-O, alive, alive-O,
Crying cockles and mussels, alive, alive-O!

## POND DIPPING

**What to take with you**
- A net or sieve for dipping
- A jam jar or container

a ram's horn snail

Children love exploring ponds and spotting the tiniest creatures as they skit around the water. Prepare to get flat on your tummies to get a close look without falling in. Fish, frogs, tadpoles and water snails are easiest to spot. Above the surface, ponds are teeming with skaters, mayflies, dragonflies and damselflies.

Fill your jam jars with water from the pond. Check to see what is already caught. Dip your net in the pond and slowly pass it through the water. Empty the net, complete with plants or creatures, into the jar and, when the contents settle, see what you have caught. Carefully empty the jars back in the pond when you have finished.

### Mayflies
These hatch in ponds, living first as an underwater grub, called a nymph. They emerge as flying creatures, living for only a few hours and quickly mating before they die.

### Diving beetles
These beetles trap bubbles of air to keep them alive underwater. They move very quickly and are exciting to watch.

### Frog spawn and tadpoles
The jelly of frog spawn contains hundreds of eggs, preparing to hatch into tadpoles. Over several weeks, limbs are formed, the tail shrinks and a frog is created. These frogs will one day

try to come back to the same pond to lay their own eggs. Toad spawn looks very different and is laid in long ribbons, not in round clusters.

Dragonflies and damselflies

These live underwater for much of their lives and it is probably the larger dragonfly nymph that you will find when pond dipping. The hatched grub crawls to the surface. As the skin dries and hardens, it splits and releases the dragonfly to the air, coming back to the pond for drinking or to lay eggs.

Pond skater

pond skater

The surface tension of the water is enough to keep these tiny creatures skimming along the top of the pond, sharing the weight load across each of its skinny, long legs.

a common pond snail

to the railway line. At the wooden gate ahead, you get your first sighting of Hadleigh Castle.

The path carries straight on, through a flat meadow with woods and trees up to your left. There is a fingerpost pointing the way to Hadleigh Castle, 2.4 km / 1.5 miles away. Just before the next gate is a small, deep pond with frogs and ducks.

**4** A fenced pond dipping area is on your right. This is a great place to stop for a while, watching for frogs, dragonflies, pond skaters and water snails. A wooden walkway makes it easy.

Carry on through the next meadow, with open marshy land on your right. The castle has now disappeared from view, but reveals itself gloriously as the path gently bends at the far end of the meadow.

**5** Pass through the kissing gates, through a field and over a stile on a well-marked footpath. Walk along the edge of an arable field to a stile at the foot of the castle hill.

**6** Over the stile, turn left and climb up the hill. The entrance to the castle is at the very top, the other side of the five bar gate. Look behind you for long views of the flat Essex marshes to the sea. Watch for birds; sea birds and marshland birds, and kestrels flying overhead. It is the perfect strategic position for protecting the Thames estuary and access to the city of London.

Scramble over the castle ruins. Often deserted in the week and filled with picnicking families and kite flyers at weekends.

**7** Head out on the path between the two towers. Defy any children not to run all the way down the gently rolling ridge to the fields below. Climb over the stile at the foot of the hill and follow the well-defined path straight on through the fields and then woods, coming out after half a mile or so at Leigh-on-Sea.

**8** Turn right down the main road, passing the station. Turn right here, crossing over the railway line and down the steps to the sea front. This way in to Old Leigh avoids the main road and takes you past the cockle sheds and boats. Stop at one of the

crowded but good pubs on the way or cut on to the high street to Kym's Tea Garden and have a more civilised ice cream, simple hot food, sandwiches and cakes.

**9** Head through the old town to the small beach to while away some time making sandcastles, paddling or squelching bare feet in estuary mud if the tide is out. Stop to watch the fishermen unloading their catch at the end of the day. Pick up fish and chips at the Mayflower takeaway right by the beach and eat them there and then or on the train on the way home.

**Eat Me, Drink Me**
- Kym's Tea Garden, 64 High Street, Old Leigh, Essex. Tel 01702 477315 or online at www.kymsteagarden.co.uk. Last hot food served at 4.30 p.m. Open all week from 10 a.m. to 4 p.m. in winter, 10 a.m. to 5 p.m. in summer.
- The Crooked Billet Pub, 51 High Street, Leigh-on-Sea, Essex. Tel 01702 480289.
- The Peterboat, 27 High Street, Leigh-on-Sea, Essex. Tel 01702 475666.
- Right next to the beach at the far end of the town is Mayflower Old Leigh Traditional Fish & Chips, 5 High Street, Leigh-on-Sea, Essex. Tel 01702 480930.

**Useful Information**
- For Hadleigh Country Park information call 01702 551072 or visit www.essexcc.gov.uk.
- For the local RSPB website with details on nearby sightings visit www.southendrspb.co.uk.
- For information on the Essex Wildlife Trust visit www.essexwt.org.uk.
- For information about Hadleigh Castle and online shopping for wooden bows and arrows, catapults and crossbows and fancy dress knights and princesses visit www.english-heritage.co.uk.

**Did you know?**
- The *Mayflower* that took the Pilgrim Fathers to New England in the USA is thought to be originally from Leigh-on-Sea. It is registered in the London Port Book of 1606 as the Mayflower of Leigh, by its Master, Robert Bonner of Leigh.
- The six wives of Henry VIII were, in order, Catherine of Aragon, Anne Boleyn, Jane Seymour, Anne of Cleves, Catherine Howard and Catherine Parr. Repeat this mnemonic to remember their fates: divorced, beheaded, died; divorced, beheaded, survived.

# 24. From Pudding Lane to St Paul's cathedral

The City of London

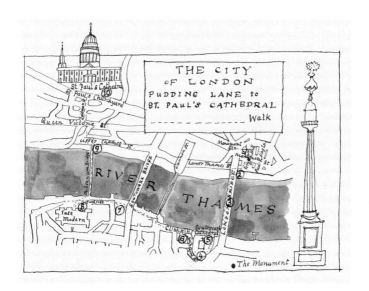

**The Adventure**

See and learn about some of the City of London's greatest landmark buildings, some of which are very old and some very new. We will be taking in the Monument, London Bridge, Southwark Cathedral, Borough Market, the *Golden Hinde*, the Clink, the Globe Theatre, Tate Modern, the Millennium Bridge and St Paul's Cathedral. This gives you ample opportunity to do all sorts of different things: you could climb the Monument and learn about the Great Fire of London, find Shakespeare's tomb, explore a food market, be a pirate on board a galleon, get spooked in an old prison, imagine you are an Elizabethan thespian, discover international modern art in an old power station, walk on the 'wobbly' bridge and if you've got any puff left you can send a secret message to a conspirator in the Whispering Gallery at St Paul's Cathedral. If the tide is out you can go mudlarking along the shore of the River Thames looking for treasure.

**Map** *London A–Z*

**Distance** The walk is about 2 km / 1.2 miles but the distance will depend on how many of the attractions you visit along the way.

**Terrain** London pavements which can be quite hard on the legs

### What will I need?
- Some pocket money for postcards of the places you visit to make a scrapbook of your day
- For mudlarking you'll need a good pair of boots and rubber gloves, a plastic bag, information about the tides (see the Port of London Authority website, see page 186) and a Port of London Authority licence if you want to dig or use a metal detector.

### How to get there
Travel to Monument tube station. For information call Transport for London on 0207 222 1234 or vist www.tfl.gov.uk.

### What can we listen to on the way?
- *Selections from the Diary of Samuel Pepys* read by Michael Maloney (Naxos)

## LONDON'S BURNING
London's burning, London's burning,
Fetch the engines, Fetch the engines,
Fire, fire! Fire, fire!
Pour on water, pour on water.

## Walk the Walk

**1** From Monument tube station walk in an easterly direction along Monument Street and you will see the Monument, located on the junction of Monument Street and Fish Street Hill. Built to commemorate the Great Fire of London in 1666 it was designed by Sir Christopher Wren and built out of Portland stone with a copper urn topped by flames symbolising the Great Fire. It took six years to build and is 61.5 m / 202 feet tall, the exact distance from where the Monument is sited to where the fire started in Pudding Lane. It is the tallest isolated stone column in the world. You get a fantastic 360° view of London if you climb the 311 steps to the top and you get a certificate to prove it.

**2** Head down Fish Street Hill, cross Lower Thames Street (the church, St Magnus the Martyr opposite, once formed part of the roadway approach to the old London Bridge). Turn right and then turn left following a sign to 'London Bridge via steps'. Climb the stairs and follow signs to the west side so that you come out on to the bridge on the correct side. Come up the steps.

**3** Cross the River Thames over London Bridge with fantastic views up and down the river: look out for Tower Bridge, HMS *Belfast*, the Oxo Tower, Canary Wharf, BT Tower, St Paul's Cathedral, the *Golden Hinde*, and the 'gherkin'. See if you can find the symbol of the City of London (two dragons holding a shield with a red cross and sword on it) on the bridge anywhere. How many Wren churches can you spot? Sing a round of 'London's Burning' and 'Oranges and Lemons'.

**4** Just before you get to the end of the bridge take the steps on the right down to Pickfords Wharf, a cobbled street. Turn right and then left past the Mudlark Tavern. Pick your way round to the right towards Southwark Cathedral into Green Dragon Court. There has been a church on this site for over a thousand years. The main structure of the cathedral was built in 1220–1420 and it was designated a cathedral in 1905. Go in and see if you can find Shakespeare's tomb. Exit via the gate next to the main entrance of the cathedral. Directly opposite you will see Borough Market, one of the best food markets in London (Thursday, Friday and Saturdays only), where you can pick up something to eat. Afterwards leave the market where you entered and with your back to it head straight down Cathedral Street to the river.

**5** Just ahead is the *Golden Hinde*, an exact replica of the sixteenth-century warship that Sir Francis Drake made his epic round-the-world voyage in. The current galleon was built in 1973 and has also sailed round the world. It is now in dry dock and you are allowed on board. (See page 186)

**6** Walk down Clink Street past the remains of the thirteenth-century Winchester Palace where the Bishops of Winchester lived until 1814 when it burnt down. All that remains is the rose window in the west gable end. Just beyond this is The Clink, a once

## ORANGES AND LEMONS
Oranges and lemons
Say the bells of St Clement's
You owe me five farthings
Say the bells of St Martin's
When will you pay me?
Say the bells of Old Bailey
When I grow rich
Say the bells of Shoreditch
When will that be?
Say the bells of Stepney
I do not know
Says the great bell of Bow
Here comes the chopper to chop off your head
Here comes the candle to light you to bed!

notorious prison from 1151–1780 and the source of the expression 'in the clink'. It has now been done out as a ghoulish tourist attraction. Turn right just beyond here past Wagamama into Bank End. Take in the fantastic view of St Paul's Cathedral across the river.

**7** Continue walking with the Thames on your right, through a tunnel under Southwark Bridge beyond which you will find a plethora of restaurants to choose from for lunch. (See page 185 for suggestions.) Otherwise find somewhere with a good river view to have your picnic. From here it is a short walk to the Globe Theatre. Opened in 1997, it was built to replace the original theatre that burnt down in 1613. The theatre caught fire during a performance of *Henry VIII* when a theatrical cannon, set off during the performance, misfired, lighting the wooden beams and thatching. It was rebuilt but closed down by Puritans in 1642 and subsequently knocked down for tenement buildings. This new building, the brainchild of American filmmaker Sam

Wanamaker, is a copy of the theatre as it would have been in the Elizabethan time when Shakespeare was working here. The theatre is as historically accurate as it could be. 'Green' oak was cut and shaped according to Elizabethan ways, the walls covered in a white lime wash and the roof made of water reed thatch. There are seats but most of the space is standing room only and open air. It is reputedly the first thatched roof to be permitted in London since the Great Fire of London. We recommend you take a 'pop in' tour. A full tour might be overkill at this stage. You may want

## MUDLARKING

Be an amateur archaeologist at low tide on the River Thames, looking for treasure among the shingle and silt. Climb down the steps near Tate Modern. If you want to dig or use a metal detector, get a permit from The Port of London Authority. This will allow you to dig up to a depth of 7.5 cm. If you just want to sift through the top layer of mud, without digging, you will not need a licence. The Thames foreshore is archeologically rich. It has historically been an important transport route so you can, if you're lucky, find Roman, medieval and Elizabethan treasures. If you do find something of potential merit it must be taken to the Museum of London for identification and recording.

to just walk past and admire the exterior architecture. The original Globe Theatre had twenty sides.

**8** Just ahead are the Millennium Bridge and Tate Modern. Visit the latter first. Formally a power station, designed by architect Sir Giles Gilbert Scott in 1947, it was converted by the Swiss architects Herzog and De Meuron and reopened in May 2000. It is home to international modern art and in 2012 will open a glass pyramid extension to house photography. The chimney is an imposing part of the London skyline and is capped by a coloured light feature by artist Michael Craig-Martin. If you want to go mudlarking, here is the place to do it, just down by the river.

**9** Now cross the Millennium Bridge, a pedestrian-only steel suspension bridge, designed by architects Foster and Partners, sculptor Sir Anthony Caro and engineers Arup. This new footbridge opened in June 2000 but was closed three days later as bilateral vibrations caused the bridge to sway, hence the nickname 'wobbly bridge'. The bridge cost over £18 million to build. You get fantastic views up and down the Thames as well as one of the best views of St Paul's Cathedral.

**10** Continue on to St Paul's Cathedral. Designed by Sir Christopher Wren and built between1675 and 1710, the original having been destroyed by the Great Fire, St Paul's is built in the shape of a cross and the golden coloured ball and lantern on the top is 108.4 m / 355 feet high. The funerals of Lord Nelson, the first Duke of Wellington and Sir Winston Churchill were held here.

### Eat Me, Drink Me
- Take your pick from a number of riverside restaurants. For something a bit more unusual, we liked the Anatolian restaurant Tas Pide, 20–22 New Globe Walk. Tel 020 7928 3300 or online at www.tasrestaurant.com.
- If not, pick up a hamburger or another delicacy from Borough Market. www.boroughmarket.org.uk

### Useful Information
- The Monument. For information call 020 7401 5000 or go to www.cityoflondon.gov.org or www.towerbridge.org.uk.

- Southwark Cathedral. For information call 020 7367 6700 or go to www.southwark.anglican.org/cathedral.
- The *Golden Hinde*. Tel 020 7403 0123 or online at www.goldenhinde.org. Open 10 a.m. to 5.30 p.m. weekdays, and 10 a.m. to 5 p.m. at weekends unless busy with education activities or special events.
- The Clink Prison Museum. For information call 020 7403 0900 or visit www.clink.co.uk.
- The Globe. For more information call 020 7401 9919 or online at www.shakespeares-globe.org.uk.
- Tate Modern. For information call 020 7401 5000 or online at www.tate.org.uk.
- Borough Market. Visit www.boroughmarket.org.uk.
- St Paul's Cathedral. For more information visit www.stpauls.co.uk.
- Port of London Authority. Tel 0207 743 7900 or online at www.portoflondon.co.uk. Permits cost £7.50 per day and can be obtained by calling 01474 562 200.
- Museum of London. For information call 0870 444 3852 or online at www.museumoflondon.org.uk.

### Did you know?
- Sir Christopher Wren was hauled up and down in a basket to inspect the works whilst St Paul's Cathedral was being built.
- The word mudlark was originally used for desperately poor East End children in Victorian London who scoured the Thames foreshore for bits of coal, rope, discarded iron, copper nails, old bones and tools to earn a few pennies. 'Toshers' scavenged in sewers and 'grubbers' in drains.

### Rainy Day Options
- Run between the various places and linger inside rather than out.

# 25. Sense and Sensibility

Jane Austen in Chawton, Hampshire

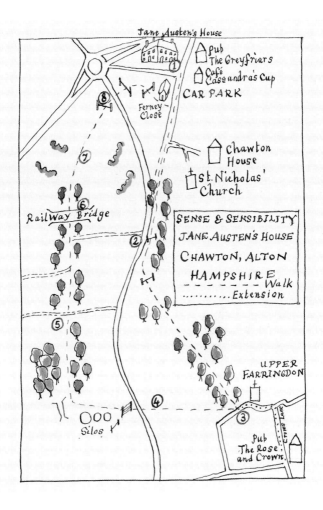

## The Adventure

This is a visit to Chawton in Hampshire and the house where Jane Austen lived, with her mother and sister, for the last eight years of her life. Jane and her family moved to Chawton because her brother, Edward, inherited the estate here. The house Jane lived in is late seventeenth century and as you step through the door you are instantly immersed in her world with its low ceilings, panelled doors, decor and good collection of personal effects: jewellery, furniture, letters, portraits and items of clothing. It is hard to believe that from the tiny writing table in the dining parlour Austen revised her manuscripts for *Sense and Sensibility* and *Pride and Prejudice* and subsequently wrote *Mansfield Park, Emma* and *Persuasion*.

We will be taking a path out of the village past the church where Jane would have worshipped and walking to Upper Farringdon, a trip Jane would have done often as she was particularly friendly with the curate's family, the Revd John Benn. If you don't have time to pick up the audio books before you leave home they are on sale at the house.

**Map** Ordnance Survey Explorer Map 133

**Distance** 5 km / 3 miles with a half-mile detour into Upper Farringdon

**Terrain** Easy walking across fields that can get waterlogged after rain. Otherwise it's good paths all the way.

## What will I need?
- A notebook to make notes for your own novel
- Watercolour paints and paper
- A copy of *Sense and Sensibility* or *Emma*

## How to get there
Take the M3 to Junction 5. At the first roundabout take the A30.

Then first left on the A287 signposted Farnham. At the roundabout take the B3349 to Alton and keep going. Don't go through the centre of Alton. At the T-junction turn right, signposted (A31) M3, then turn left to Alton and the A31. Go under a railway bridge, turn right and then left. From here follow the brown heritage signs to Jane Austen's house. Look out for a turning on the right and another brown sign. Come into Chawton and drive to the centre of the village, past the Greyfriars Inn and park in the car park just beyond it on the left. Jane Austen's house is opposite.

## What can we listen to on the way?
• *Jane Austen Collection volumes I* and *II* read by Juliet Stevenson (Naxos)

## Walk the Walk
**1** Once you've looked round the house, cross the road, turn right and walk down the dead-end lane past some picturesque thatched cottages and out of the village. Shortly on your left you will come to Chawton House. Turn left into the driveway and take the first right to St Nicholas' Church to see the graves of Jane's mother and sister (Jane is buried in Winchester Cathedral). Come back to the path and turn left back on to the road. As it peters out into a track follow it through the trees, parallel to the road.

**2** At the stile and DEFRA sign, climb over and then on to and over another stile and keep going for

some distance. At the third stile follow the fingerpost diagonally across the meadow heading towards some trees and another stile. Climb over and follow the footpath up through some beautiful fields, and on into an avenue of wellingtonia trees followed by an avenue of yew trees and down a hill towards the houses of Upper Farringdon.

**3** At the crossroads you have a choice:

**A** If you want to eat at the Rose and Crown pub in Upper Farringdon, turn left here. It was Jane's brother Edward who converted these from almshouses into a pub in 1810. Walk past the farm buildings and right just past the barn, past the church and down to the lane. Turn left and then right down Crows Lane all the way to the Rose and Crown. Afterwards retrace your steps to this crossroads and keep going straight ahead.

**B** If you are not going to the pub, turn right at the crossroads and walk along the gravelly track gently downhill, past hedges of elderflower until you get to the road.

**4** At the A32 do be careful of traffic. Cross over and head for a metal five bar gate slightly to your right. Climb the stile. Veer round the right-hand side of some agricultural silos into a field. Walk round the left-hand edge of the field and then into the trees. Turn right on to a disused railway track. Walk straight ahead.

**5** Go straight at the crossroads, ignoring paths to the left and right.

**6** Walk under a railway bridge.

**7** Further on the track turns to the left but the actual footpath goes straight across the field ahead. The path bends round the edge

### GENTEEL AMUSEMENTS

- Work up an Austen-style plot with your own romantic heroine and a dashing young man as you walk along.
- Take up some genteel pursuits and take along watercolours to paint wild flowers, trees, the church and the house.
- Design costumes for your cast of characters.

## From Chapter XVIII of *Sense and Sensibility*
### by Jane Austen

Edward returned to them with fresh admiration of the surrounding country; in his walk to the village he had seen many parts of the valley to advantage; and the village itself, in a much higher situation than the cottage, afforded a general view of the whole, which had exceedingly pleased him. This was a subject which ensured Marianne's attention; and she was beginning to describe her own admiration of these scenes, and to question him more minutely on the objects that had particularly struck him, when Edward interrupted her by saying, 'You must not enquire too far, Marianne; remember I have no knowledge in the picturesque, and I shall offend you by my ignorance and want of taste if we come to particulars. I shall call hills steep, which ought to be bold; surfaces strange and uncouth, which ought to be irregular and rugged; and distant objects out of sight, which ought only to be indistinct through the soft medium of a hazy atmosphere. You must be satisfied with such admiration as I can honestly give. I call it a very fine country, – the hills are steep, the woods seem full of fine timber, and the valley looks comfortable and snug, – with rich meadows and several neat farm houses scattered here and there. It exactly answers my idea of a fine country.'

of the field to the right and downhill. At the trees follow the footpath to the left. At the edge of the trees climb over the stile and turn right. Walk along the edge of the field and over the stile at the bottom.

**8** Cross the main road, then go up some steps and over another stile. Walk towards the houses with the line of trees on your right. Go over the stile. Walk down past the houses into Ferney Close and on to the lane ahead. Turn left and walk back into the village and to your car.

### Eat Me, Drink Me

- Cassandra's Cup, The Hollies, Winchester Road, Chawton, Hampshire. Tel 01420 83144. Open from 10.30 a.m. to 4.30 p.m. May to September, open Wednesday to Sunday. April, October and November, open Thursday to Sunday. March and December, open Friday to Sunday. February, open Saturday and Sunday. They close the last Sunday before Christmas and re-open the first Saturday in February. They always open on bank holiday Mondays but are closed the subsequent Wednesday. This tea shop provides a variety of home-cooked food, homemade cakes, oven-baked jacket potatoes and toasted sandwiches.
- The Greyfriars, Winchester Road, Chawton, Hampshire. Tel 01420 83841 or online at www.thegreyfriars.co.uk.
- The Rose and Crown, Crows Lane, Upper Farringdon, Alton, Hampshire. Tel 01420 588231 or go to www.farringdon.biz. A really nice pub that has delicious food and offers accommodation.

### Useful Information

- Jane Austen's House, Chawton, Alton, Hampshire. Tel 01420 83262 or online at www.jane-austens-house-museum.org.uk.

They have quizzes for children and an annual competition. Open January and February Saturday and Sunday plus February half-term from 10.30 a.m. to 4.30 p.m. Open March to May daily from 10.30 a.m. to 4.30 p.m. Open June to August daily from 10 a.m. to 5 p.m. Open September to December daily and January 1st from 10.30 a.m. to 4.30 p.m.

- The Jane Austen Society fosters appreciation and study of Jane Austen's life and helps maintain the house at Chawton. For more information visit www.janeaustensoci.freeuk.com.
- For information about a permanent exhibition in Bath and the six years she spent there visit www.janeausten.co.uk.
- Get a charming Regency cut-out doll to dress in clothes just like those worn by Jane Austen at www.englishvillagedesigns.co.uk.
- Read *Cassandra's Sister*, a portrait of the young life of Jane Austen by Veronica Bennett.

**Did you know?**
- The original name for *Sense and Sensibility* was *Elinor and Marianne*.
- Jane Austen's first novel, *Northanger Abbey*, sold for £10 in 1803.

**Rainy Day Options**
- Gilbert White's House, Selborne, Hampshire. Tel 01420 511275 or online at www.gilbertwhiteshouse.org.uk. After looking round Austen's house you could drive to Selborne and visit the Revd Gilbert White's house. Jane was familiar with White (he was also a vicar at Upper Farringdon at some point) and visited Selborne. White was a naturalist and a pioneer in the interdependence of animals and plants in nature. The original manuscript for *Natural History and Antiquities of Selborne* is on view at the house, which has been renovated in period style using descriptions from White's letters.

# A YEAR IN THE LIFE

Seasons come and go and each walk can look and feel very different at different times of year. Explore in all seasons: enjoy the berries, hips and fungi of autumn; the wild daffodils and bluebells of spring; the poppies, daisies, and bright meadow flowers of summer; and the snowdrops, catkins and mistletoe of winter.

## January
Alder
Hazel catkins
Wild snowdrops
Winter wading birds such as teal
   and grey plover
Robins

## February
Coltsfoot
Celandines
Winter aconites
Pussy willow
Skylarks singing
Elms in flower
Lambing starts

## March
Kingcup, sometimes called marsh
   marigold
Holly blue butterflies
Brimstone butterflies
Lesser celandine flowers
Early primroses
Nightingales and yellowhammer

birds return to England
Sugarbeet and onions planted in
   the fields
Toads move back to home ponds
Hares box in the fields

## April
Wild daffodils
Blackthorn flowers
Frogs, toads and
   newts spawn in ponds
Cowslips and oxlips
Badger cubs born
Returning birds such as chiffchaff

Common Frog

## May
Swallows return
Cow parsley in meadows
Apple tree blossom
Hawthorn blossom (mayflower)
Bluebells
Common blue butterflies
Early purple orchid

### June

Butterflies, bees
*Rosa canina* – dog rose
Foxgloves
Yellow iris (flag iris) especially in
    wet ground
Oil seed rape harvest
Ox-eye daisies
Sulphur clover flowers
Bee orchids
Water vole and otter
Common spotted orchid

### July

Wild heath (heathers)
Willowherb
Dragonflies near water
Wheat, barley and onion harvested
Bats flying in the early evening
Stag beetles flying on warm
    evenings

Long-eared bat

### August

Blackberries
Common blue butterflies
Peacock butterflies
Red admiral butterflies

### September

Alder seed/cones
Whitebeam berries
Starlings gathering in the sky
Swifts on telegraph lines

### October

Autumn colour – spindle berry
    (*Euonymus europaeus*)
Guelder rose – berries
Hedgehogs hibernate
Deciduous trees lose their leaves

### November

Birds such as coots and ducks
    gather in flocks during winter on
    lakes and ponds
Bulrushes

### December

Lots of berries are ripe at this time
    of year: berries, hips and haws
Look for holly berries, hawthorn
    berries
Mistletoe

## WILD FLOWERS

Help your children to learn the names of flowers in the hedgerows, meadows and fields. Make a game of it by seeing how many varieties of white flowers or blue flowers etc you can find. Inspire them by doing art projects when you get home. Pick up falllen petals and press between the pages of a book. Make your own flower fairy pictures and rhymes. As you are not supposed to pick wild flowers, take a camera to record your finds or sketch them in the field. Note down the flowers you've seen and where and when you've seen them.

Bluebell woods

Bird's-foot trefoil

Black mustard

Blackberry blossom

Bluebells and campion

Buttercups

Cat's ear

Catkins

Comfrey

Cow parsley

Cowslips

Dock leaves

Dog rose

197

Early purple orchid

Elderflower

Forget-me-not

Foxglove

Giant hogweed

Gorse

Grasses

Harebell

Hawkweed

Horse chestnut candle

Ox-eye daisies

Poppies

Ramsons (wild garlic)

Red campion

Rosehip

Shepherd's clock

Silverweed

Speedwell

Stitchwort

Sweet chestnut

Teasel

Yellow flag iris

Thistle

Yellow archangel

# RECIPES FOR COOKING FROM THE WILD

## Elderflower cordial

INGREDIENTS

25 elderflower heads
2 litres / 3 pints water
1 kg / 2 lb caster sugar
2 unwaxed lemons
75 g / 2½ oz citric acid
  (available from chemist shops)

You will need some sterilised bottles to put your elderflower cordial into once you have made it.

- Shake the flower heads to get rid of any creepy crawlies and place in a large bowl.
- Put the water and sugar in to a saucepan. Bring to the boil, stir and gently simmer until all the sugar has melted. To check, dip a wooden spoon into the mixture and see if there are any sugar granules on it when you pull it out.
- Peel off the lemon zest in fairly wide strips and then cut the lemon into slices. Place the zest and lemon slices into the bowl with the elderflowers.
- Get a grown-up to pour the boiling syrup into the bowl of elderflowers.
- Stir in the citric acid.
- Leave for twenty-four hours.

- Pour the liquid through a muslin-lined sieve and bottle.
- You will need to mix your cordial with water to taste – it is particularly good with fizzy water, ice and a sprig of mint.

## Dandelion salad

These are one of the most common weeds in Britain. They flower in late spring but the leaves can be gathered at almost any time of the year. To make a salad pick the youngest leaves, trim the stalk and wash well. Chop the leaves and mix with a dressing. Delicious.

Dandelion.

## Wild rose petal jam

INGREDIENTS

220 g / ½ lb jam-making sugar
300 ml / ½ pint water
The juice of one large lemon
220 g / ½ lb wild rose petals

You will need some sterilised jam jars to put your jam in and some wax seals, lids and labels.

- Put the sugar and water in a pan and bring to the boil. Stir and simmer gently until all the sugar is completely dissolved.

- Add the lemon juice and stir.
- Add the rose petals, stir and continue to simmer.
- Keep going until the 'setting point' is reached. You can test this by putting a little bit on a cold saucer, then pushing it with your finger. If it forms a wrinkly skin it is ready.
- After you have left the jam to cool for a few minutes pour it into your clean warmed jars (if the jars are cold they might crack because the jam mixture will be very hot). Put on the wax seals, the lids and write a label.

*dog rose*

## Nettle tea

Put some nettles in a pot, cover with water (quantity depends on how strong you like your cup of tea) and bring to the boil until the water is coloured slightly green. Take out the nettles, pour the tea into a cup and add a slice of lemon. Watch carefully as the tea turns bright pink!

## Nettle soup

INGREDIENTS
50 g / 2 oz butter
1 onion

2 medium potatoes
500 ml / 1 pint
   vegetable stock
Three generous handfuls of young stinging nettle leaves, gathered from the top of the plants. Remember to wear gloves when picking them.
200 ml / ⅓ pint single cream
Salt and pepper

*Nettle.*

- Melt the butter in a pan.
- Finely chop the onion and cook until clear.
- Add the peeled and cubed potatoes and stir for a few minutes to glaze them with the butter.
- Add the vegetable stock and simmer for ten minutes.
- Add the chopped-up nettles and stew for a few minutes until they have wilted.
- Add the cream and some salt and pepper to taste.

## Whortleberry pie

De-stalk the whortleberries and lay them in a shallow pie dish. Sprinkle with sugar and add a drop of fruit juice. Roll out some shortcrust pastry and place on top. Brush on some milk and a sprinkling of sugar. Put in a hot oven until golden brown.

# HOUSE HUNTING

You will be amazed how many different types of building and styles of architecture there are. Every county has its own architectural vernacular, often dictated by the materials available nearby, (flint, sandstone, wood, thatch) as much as the period in history when they were built. Look at the pictures below to help you work out which county you are in from the style of house you can see. The type of building, such as barns, oast houses, watermills can tell you if you are in the middle of farmland, near a river or close to the sea. Play games as you go along giving yourself points for different kinds of buildings. 10 points for a thatched cottage, 50 for a windmill. The person with the most points is the winner.

**1** In the east of England, particularly in Essex and Suffolk, you will see buildings made from plaster often painted a pink colour. It was traditional to paint houses in these counties with bullocks' blood, now-a-days modern paints are used.

**2** Wooden, half timber and full timber houses are typical in Essex. The wood you see on the outside of the building is literally the skeleton of the house that supports the whole building.

**3** Whitewash has been used on buildings for centuries because it was easy to make from chalk dust. This one is in Oxfordshire.

**4** Houses are often made out of local stone. Yellow limestone is a Cotswold stone that comes from near by and fades to a honey colour.

**5** A thatch-roofed cottage in Uffington, Oxfordshire. Thatch is usually made from straw, reed or heather.

**6** At the seaside, look out for boat houses. These are old boats that no longer go anywhere and have been converted into a house. They are often painted bright colours.

**7** Red bricks have been used for many years. They are a good building material because they are fireproof and hardwearing. Look out for interestingly designed chimneys. They had to be big enough for boys to climb up and clean.

**8** A half-timbered, whitewashed thatched cottage in the Fens. The material in between the timber slats is traditionally made of wattle and daub. Wattle is a lattice of wooden stakes and daub is the mixture of clay, mud, sand and dung that was slapped on top.

**9** Beach huts come in all shapes and sizes and are often painted in pretty seaside colours.

**10** Horizontal wooden boards or 'cladding' on houses near the seaside helps protect buildings from the weather. In Essex, weatherboarded houses are traditionally painted in black; in Kent they are usually in white.

**11** This Suffolk thatch roof is steeply pitched so that the rain drains off more easily.

**12** The earliest bricks were earth blocks dried in the sun. Traditionally each county would have different coloured bricks because they were made from local materials which vary in mineral content. You should see white bricks in Sussex and East Anglia, grey bricks in Oxfordshire, Berkshire and Hampshire and black bricks in Surrey, Sussex and Berkshire.

**13** This conical shaped building is an oast house. It is used for drying hops for making beer. You will see these in Kent where they grow a lot of hops.

**14** A watermill on a pond in Suffolk. Watermills have a big wheel which is pushed round by water to make power to grind grain or in some cases to generate electricity.

**15** An old Tudor black and white timber-framed building. It has 'leaded light' windows. Small pieces of glass are held together with lead because large pieces of glass were difficult and expensive to make.

**16** There are lots of different styles of windmills. See how many different shaped ones you can see. You might even see a modern-day wind turbine which are used to make electricity.

# INDEX